Edited by Caterina Corni & Sona Datta

This book has been published by Edizioni Astragalo in conjunction with Painting Freedom: Indian Modernism and its three rebels an exhibition organised at Leicester Museum and Art Gallery, 53 New Walk, Leicester, United Kingdom LE1 7EA

11 September 2021 to 21 November 2021

Printed by
DESI Group Srl - Trecate (No) Italy

ISBN N 978-88-945920-8-5

Front cover
Untitled (Jagadharti),
Oil on canvas, 76 x 61 cm

Painting Freedom:
Indian Modernism and its three rebels

edited by
Caterina Corni
Sona Datta

Painting Freedom tells the story of Indian modern art between 1870 and 1950. Convinced that Indian artists were incapable of true "fine art", the British set up art schools in the mid-19th century. The Government College of Art in Calcutta was "established by a benevolent government for the purpose of revealing to the Indians the superiority of European art". Indian artists were encouraged to paint Indian subjects using Western standards of beauty and art practices.

By the turn of the twentieth century, however, artists in Calcutta began to question: what is Indian modern art? How could they stand apart from western conceptions of art, while also differentiating from India's own rich artistic legacy to produce something that was simultaneously Modern and Indian?

Against the backdrop of aristocratic Early Bengal oil paintings, village scrolls, and urban Kalighat paintings, emerged the nationalist Bengal School of Art.
This period coincided with the prologue to agitation for Indian Independence. Out of this tumultuous period, the enduring legacy of Modern Indian Art was produced by three artistic rebels: Hemendranath Mazumdar, Jamini Roy, and Rabindranath Tagore, who each charted a unique path in their quest to become both Indian and Modern.

The Aesthetics of Contamination

Caterina Corni

"We must remember that all artistic operations were originally rites, and that the purpose of the rite [...] is to sacrifice the old and to bring into being the new and more perfect man"

Ananda Kentish Coomaraswamy[1]

The concept of cross-contamination has become increasingly relevant. Cross-contamination (that is, cross-pollination, exchange, or *métissage*) is always the result of an encounter between cultures or between cultural forms. This is a process that very much holds a central position in historical cultures. The pathways of acculturation were always active in these cultures: their borders, precisely because they existed and were enforced, became increasingly porous and provide the fabric for encounter and exchange. Cultures can go through moments of closure, defence and autarky (for example the development of the Bengal School, and its fierce determination to regain possession of Indian artistic and cultural roots[2]). However there are also moments of openness, a desire for exchange and discovering diversity. In the second instance – one of openness and exchange – the thing that is being sought in difference/otherness through encounter and exchange, is precisely this cross-contamination. A culture is built from the proximity and exchange between two cultures that come into contact and that cross-contaminate each other: with loans, re-orientations and hybridization of identities (or parts of them).

Anthropologists tell us that this is something that has always happened.
As the scholar Alain Daniélou reminds us in his seminal essay Shiva and Dionysius[3]: "The divine is defined in the Upanishads as *"that in which opposites coexist"*". He was the brother of a cardinal, an extraordinary and controversial figure who converted to Shaivite Hinduism. It is significant that we also find a similar definition in Heraclitus - *coincidentia oppositorum* (The union of opposites), and Nicholas of Cusa considered this same union to be "the least imperfect definition of God."

The nineteenth and twentieth centuries saw the blossoming of global communications, and this was a period when Indian painting began to welcome certain trends from modern Western painting, something which had also happened to a degree in architecture. In fact, the foundations for the development of lasting mutual influences - both cultural and artistic - had already been established at the beginning of the eighteenth century, when the East India Company consolidated its trade on Indian territory, paving the way for the future British Raj. Thus, facilitated by a kind of forced coexistence, Western painters found a source of inspiration in exotic Indian landscapes while, in India, there was an increase in the tendency to create purely Western-style oil portraits[4]

The sensitivity of Indian artists was clearly affected by the historical events in the country, and they were among the earliest to have first hand experience of what the West was importing and imposing, as they were required to produce work in the style of European art and experimentation. Many European artists embarked for India seeking a totally new dimension, not only bringing with them techniques and studies from their own tradition, but also ready to embrace what India could offer. Just as modern tourists rely on a good camera, so these explorers decided to hire native painters, entrusting them with the complex task of capturing images for them. These fantastic panoramas, with their flora and fauna, brought the world an idea of India, one that would live on in Europe for many years. A new genre of painting, the Company School, was born to satisfy the taste of these new English clients. The officials of the East India Company were interested in paintings that could capture the exotic and picturesque aspects of India, but these had to be strictly painted according to European canons, using techniques such as chiaroscuro and perspective which were hitherto practically unknown to the Indian artists[5]. The artists also changed their materials, abandoning the use of gouache for example, to create a hybrid form of painting which had neither a claim to European academic naturalism nor the freedom and stylization of the previous Indian miniatures.

Furthermore, in 1854 the East India Company officially started a project to 'improve' the taste of Indian artists, regarding it as an essential moral commitment. This is how academies and art societies became a tool for disseminating English academic art in an even more fruitful way. Art schools were initially inaugurated in three of the main colonial cities: Calcutta, Mumbai and Madras, to educate local artisans. The institution of these academies brought about a social revolution in India: the artists of the time elevated their status from court artists to socially independent individuals[6]. But let's take a few steps back, and look instead at what the influences of Indian culture were on the European world.

William Jones was a puisne judge, philologist and orientalist. In 1784 he founded the Asiatic Society, he also published the translation of the play Śakuntalā by Kālidāsa, one of the greatest Indian poets (this was published in 1789 in Calcutta and in 1790 in London). Jones had first translated the play from Bengali into Latin and, subsequently, from Latin into English[7]. The work was received with great enthusiasm not only in England, but also in Germany, the Netherlands, France and Italy.

The naturalist, journalist and travel writer, Georg Forster, an eclectic and versatile character, came across the text in London. A man of great vision, he immediately understood the value of the work and above all the importance it could have for the educated public and the literary world in Germany. Śakuntalā found enormous resonance particularly with the philosophical-literary sphere, giving rise to an aesthetic discussion that included thinkers such as Herder, Schiller and Goethe. Schiller saw some aspects of an ideal classicism in Śakuntalā, which was not to be found in the ancient Greco-Roman tradition. He stated: "*In all of Greek antiquity there is no poetic representation of a beautiful femininity and a beautiful love that can even remotely compare with* Śakuntalā".[8] The relationship between these two cultures has long history. According to the critic and writer Friedrick Schlegel, Sanskrit is the perfect language[9], and the languages that derived from it represent successive stages of a progressive decline. Schlegel found himself disgusted by European materialism and rationalism, and was deeply attracted to Indian spirituality from the very start. India played a determining role in the imagination of German romantics: it embodied everything that was lacking in that precise historical moment in the West. The warm, dreamy land of poetry corresponded to the romantic's longing for a sense of unity and wholeness. India became the antithesis of the cold and prosaic Europe of the Enlightenment. The romantic interest for India was, therefore, directly proportional to the criticism the romantics levelled at the present, the West and Europe of the time. The romantics deplored the pursuit of economic profit, cold and petty rationality, the loss of faith and spiritual blindness.[10]

The concept of contamination finds even more fertile ground in painting, an art form which - as Rabindranath Tagore states - does not need any translation precisely because of its ability to speak a universal language. This makes it the ideal aesthetic field in which to gauge the success of contamination itself, its expressive power and its formal permanence. The myriad of images that this contamination gave rise to, with its open pluralism and cross pollination, seems to offer an ideal form, from both the perspective of the viewer and that of the artist, providing a guide and establishing the norms at the same time. This concept reached its peak in the unique works known as Early Bengal Oils, which gave rise to an experimentation based on the heterogeneity of languages.

Developed in the state of Bengal between the mid-nineteenth century and the beginning of the twentieth century at the behest of the aristocratic class, this quickly became an art form in its own right. The growing demand meant that European artists were busy creating paintings with Indian themes, but using Western techniques and styles. This meant that painters of the local miniaturist schools were taken on as studio apprentices.

These same painters, having learned the fundamentals, in turn helped to spread this new language. These paintings, with their bright colours and surprising pictorial compositions, are recognized among the greatest creations of Indian painting. Let us consider the work "Krishnalila" (pp. 70-71). The Sanskrit feminine noun līlā means "game", "recreation" or "pastime", but also "grace", "charm", "mere appearance" or "simulation". This can be considered one of the most representative iconographic themes. Krishna and his mistress Radha, robed in jewels and courtly clothes, are seated beneath a temple that is clearly of Mughal origin. The concept of perspective is absent, both from an architectural point of view and in the representation of the figures in the foreground and background. In the upper part of the temple a curtain is drawn back to reveal the scene to the viewer, a detail that could be seen as a subtle reference to Italian fifteenth/sixteenth-century painting, in works such as "The dream of Constantine" by Piero Della Francesca (1460 ca.) or the "Sistine Madonna" by Raphael (1513/14) where the curtain has an almost theatrical connotation. The Gopis, the shepherdesses of the village and playmates of the young Krishna, are represented harmoniously flowing through the space surrounding the two lovers. Only the movement of the arms seeks to break the solid hieratic stance of the characters: together with the stiffness of their clothes, it gives them an almost sculptural connotation. This is by no means an unsophisticated representation, rather, it reveals a very refined taste. The painting brings together a distillation of oriental preciousness (note the meticulous attention to detail) with the refinement of European taste, such as the fresh aroma of naturalness in the vegetation that infuses the entire composition. The entire spatial arrangement of the canvas is dispersed in the immensity represented by the luxuriant and verdant flora which reminds us of both of Flemish painting, and, once again, the splendid floral decorations of Beato Angelico and Pisanello. From an historical-artistic point of view, we are witnessing the moment in which the new language absorbs every memory of the centuries-old Indian tradition combining it with new Western-style trends.

"Jagaddhatri" (p. 62), literally "bearer of the world", is a manifestation of the goddess Parvati. In this splendid painting she is depicted sitting on a lion (a symbol of strength) captured in the act of biting the head of a demon-elephant. The choice of monochrome painting for the background reflects the taste for the Flemish style and helps to emphasize the figure of the goddess, who almost seems to challenge the viewer with her strong and resolute gaze. Jagaddhatri and the two animals are portrayed according to a strictly pyramidal arrangement. The lines of perspective in the composition converge on the goddess, the vanishing point and symbolic centre of the scene. The characters are arranged according to proportional ratios, and are smaller than the central figure. The expressiveness of Jagaddhatri's face gives her an air that is at the same time human, maternal and warrior-like. The colours are vivid and the bright red of her dress stands out above all the others. A symbol of fertility and purity, red is the colour of Shakti (the personification of feminine strength). Indeed, all the deities who are charitable, courageous, protective and have the ability to destroy evil, wear red garments. The second focal point is the lion slaying the demon. Its white colour indicates purity, cleanliness, peace and knowledge. The vital spark of this remarkable work comes from the energy of the drawing, which stands against the background, elegant and harmonious. The goddess Tripura Sundari (p.74) sits on a lotus flower, which rests on a bed supported above the reclining figure of Sadashiva, also known as Kameshwara, the Lord of desire. Below Sadashiva, there are niches that echo the divisions seen in polyptychs. These contain four male divinities: Bhrama the creator, Vishnu the preserver, Rudra the destroyer and Shiva the Lord of Yoga. The position of the Goddess symbolizes her Supreme Power, worshiped even by those who rule the cosmos itself. With three of her four hands she holds a goad, a sugar cane bow and an arrow. The iconography shows Tripura Sundari as the power that guides Life, the Shakti of allurement and seduction that makes the world continue to turn in the circle of Samsara, the endless cycle of life. It also represents the power of the goddess to take us beyond worldly reality. Tripurasundari personifies the living, balanced female principle, one that is not ashamed, that does not submit and that can always trust that her love will effortlessly bring together Eros and spirit. The semicircle created by the finely damasked throne-bed softens the rigidly geometric composition. This is further softened by the architectural decorations, which lead the eye of the viewer towards the central scene. The robes of the goddess are rich with precious ornaments, characteristic of the Indian pictorial tradition. The painting is striking for its powerfully decorative refinement, not only in the details of the robes and jewels, but also in the background. The gold background captures all the magnificence of the goddess, and recalls the majesty of the Madonnas of Italian painting.

The history of the relationship between the West and India is one of a dialogue filled with mutual stimuli and cross pollinations. To recognize this, one simply needs the courage to go beyond clichés and seek true knowledge that is, above all, free from preconceptions.

1 - Coomaraswamy, Ananda Kentish. *Figures of Speech or Figures of Thought? The Traditional View of Art,* Luzac&Co, London 1946: 8.

2 - The Bengal School of Art, commonly known as the Bengal School, was an Indian art movement and style of painting that originated in Bengal, primarily in Calcutta and Shantiniketan. It flourished throughout the Indian subcontinent during the time of the British Raj in the early 20th century. Also known as the "Indian style of painting" it was associated with Indian nationalism (swadeshi) and led by Abanindranath Tagore (1871-1951), but was also promoted and supported by British arts administrators such as EB Havell, the principal of the Government College of Art and Craft in Calcutta from 1896.

3 - Daniélou, Alain. *Shiva and Dionysius,* Inner Traditions International, Rochester, Vermont, 1984.

4 - Lorenzetti, Tiziana. "*Modernismo EeModelli Figurativi delle Tradizioni Antiche Nelle Esperienze della Pittura Indiana di Primo Novecento.*" Rivista Degli Studi Orientali, vol. 81, no. 1/4, 2008: 127.

5 - Mitter, *Art & Nationalism in Colonial India, 1850-1922,* Cambridge University Press, 2011: 172.

6 - Trautmann, Matthias, *Wischer, Beate, Heterogenität in der Schule. Eine kritische Einführung,* Publikationen an der Universitat Bielefeld, 2011: 54

7 - Jones, William, *Sacontala or The Fatal ring, an Indian drama by Calidas,* translated from the original Sanscrit and Pracrit, Copper, Calcutta, 1789: 3. That there is also a Bengalese version is confirmed by V. Mazzarino, Bibliographic note, in Kālidāsa, il riconoscimento di Śakuntalā, edited by V. Mazzarino, Adelphi, Milan, 1943: 45.

8 - Translated from Clerici Luca, M. Meli, P. Mura, *Carmina Indica,* Padova University Press, 2015: 171.

9 - "On the Language and Wisdom of the Indians," in *The Aesthetic and Miscellaneous Works of Friedrich von Schlegel,* E. Millington (trans.), London: H. G. Bohn. 1860

10 - Helbfass Wilhelm, *India and Europe: an essay in understanding,* State University of New York Press, 1988:81-82

Freedom First: Artistic Horizons and Conceptual Responsibilities

Daniel Rycroft
Department of Art History and World Art Studies
University of East Anglia

The idea of freedom is enchanting. It is also complex, extremely complex, for it always operates at multiple scales and connects individuals to many different kinds of political, civic, artistic, utopian, and knowledge communities.[1] Freedom is also restless, always on some kind of mission and entangled, often productively, with other important yet oftentimes vexed principles, such as democracy, justice, or peace. As a shared and communicable value-system, it energises a host of social, educational, and philosophical possibilities. It becomes powerful in its ambivalent capacity either to determine or to transcend cultural identities and/or cultural differences. So, to what extent might anyone be able to claim, or even to understand, freedom whether in terms of an evolving politics of freedom (which might incorporate a responsibility to respect and protect diverse or even competing freedoms), or an evolving horizon of freedom (which might invite a deeper, more sensitive, and more pluralistic expression or evocation of freedom among its many proponents)?

The Idea of Freedom

In acknowledging that freedom has multiple meanings - whether as freedom 'from' (oppression; want; etc.) or freedom 'to' (express; associate; etc.) - freedom has crafted for itself an ambiguous and largely unseen presence in diverse lives, relationships, livelihoods, societies, constitutions, institutions, and imaginations. We all know that it exists, and that it is an important part of human experience. But typically we are not well-prepared to communicate or even to think about the basics: how it exists, and how it changes either in meaning or in texture; and what its limits are, and why it affects people differently. Does freedom have its own language, literature, or culture?

In an effort to address the complexity of 'freedom', we are drawn to the extraordinary work and vision of various philosophers, educators, and artists - such as Rabindranath Tagore, an early twentieth-century luminary - whose willingness to think of and live with freedom has enlivened its humaneness, its radicalism, and its ideational scope. In the words of a late twentieth-century American philosopher of religion, Creighton Peden, it was Tagore's ability to transform freedom - from an abstract idea into a lived ideal - that made his philosophy of freedom universal, and so we can first acknowledge, and then elucidate and question, different facets of this process:

The ideal which lies at the heart of Rabindranath Tagore's philosophy is Mukti, or Freedom. This freedom is not to be conceived in a narrow social or political sense; rather, it is the

heart of the spiritual endeavour which involves the deeper self. ... The Mukti or deepest freedom we seek occurs when in all our relationships we achieve Jnanam or Wisdom. To reach this goal we must continuously extend our self-knowledge, must continuously widen our experiences. ... In the deeper realm of Mukti, Jnanam is to be found, the inner harmony of conscious relationship. ... Law in the broader social realm provides the freedom of peace, but in deeper social relationships we find our freedom through Goodness or Love. ... What Tagore seeks to do is to cultivate the individual so that, on the one hand, there is an adequate adjustment of our individual life to our social life; and, on the other, the relating of these two factors to the vast needs of humanity. For this adjustment process to occur, our educational training must give emphasis to the spirit or acceptance of mutual responsibility.[2]
This process has a particular resonance and ongoing feasibility, one way or another, in the domain of the visual arts. Even if we are not artists ourselves, we still have the potential to respond actively and responsibly to the historical experience of artists involved in the making and, indeed, unmaking of different kinds of freedoms. This was certainly the case for a whole generation of modern South Asian artists in the decades before independence and partition, whose lives and worldview were impacted both by the humanism of the Bengal Renaissance and the anti-humanism of empire.[3] Exponents of the Bengal Renaissance, such as Tagore, enabled a new cultural consciousness to emerge in an era of high imperialism. Although empire, nationalism, cultural difference, universalism, humanism, knowledge, and artistic creativity all mean something quite new now, especially when compared to the previous century, the insights and processes generated then are still to be highly valued. For they tell us - sometimes directly, oftentimes more obliquely - that another world is not only possible, but also necessary and plausible.

By the early twentieth century, the Bengal Renaissance had prompted a diversity of cultural self-expression, to the extent that modern painters in India could define and develop 'freedom' singularly and in line with their own artistic tenets, most notably as a means of integrating a nascent sense of local (Bengali), national (Indian), and global (human) belonging. Yet in the realm of India's artistic modernism, freedom was rarely observed, experienced, or depicted as 'freedom' per se. For the compulsion was first to respond to the demands and tensions of combining the ideals of originality and authenticity, rather than to illustrate an imposed, superficial, abstract, or under-developed idea of freedom.

In articulating freedom as an inherent quality of (artistic) originality and (human) authenticity, the artists who aligned to the new ethos of the Santiniketan School - defined largely by Nandalal Bose and Rabindranath Tagore, as master artist and master educator respectively - soon found ways to give voice to freedom. Here, freedom emerged less as an abstract principle, and more as the practical means of developing an integrated vision: i.e. the connectivity and mutual imbrication of, for example, self and society, perception and reality, artist and image, identity and difference, home and the world.

ILLUSTRATION 1 - *Jamini Roy, Untitled (Rabindranath Tagore), (p. 289)*
This vision of connectivity both employed and extended inherited philosophical paradigms, which advocated the conceptualisation of dualities via their convergence (rather than via their distance). For example, as modern and largely urban or cosmopolitan artists and writers started to re-evaluate the Deshi (folk) elements - as being integral to India's cultural value-systems, rather than as being peripheral, or of little importance - they would also be able to enrich the overall idea of India's Marga (civilisational) culture, and vice versa. By generating this more integrated idea of India's cultural fabric, they could better educate apprentice artists and philosophers: to become proper embodiments of mediation and translation, not only between elite and non-elite domains of society but also between different facets of the self, taken individually and collectively.

Similarly, the locality of Tagore's educational or 'world' centre at Santiniketan - namely Visva Bharati - was defined by its Deshi (folk) cultures and the proximity of Adivasi (indigenous/tribal) peoples, such as Santals (or Santhals). The idea was, therefore, to develop a sustainable ethos of humanist cooperation that could, in accordance with the idealism of integration, enable minority communities to coalesce better with, and more directly contribute to, the emergent idea of new India, and vice versa.[4] The transformation of ideas into lived ideals inaugurated a departure from the colonialist construct of India as a series of distinct peoples and cultures, to procure a more holistic sense of interconnection, intertwining, and interdependence: past, present, and future.

ILLUSTRATION 2 - *Ramkinkar Baij, Untitled, (pp. 212-213)*
To a large extent, this holistic sense of social time is, or was, the freedom that informed the artistic practice of the Santiniketan School. It yielded an iconography of freedom that was, however, self-effacing. As those familiar with modern art in South Asia will attest, it was a version of freedom that was primarily artistic rather than political, for its emergence was dependent on the artistic capacity first to imagine, then to characterise, and to mediate a freedom characterised by as much by humility, locality and the present, as by modernity, the world and the future. It was a response to the quiet, indirect, and largely self-motivated call to create: itself a process that animated the wider call for artists, writers, poets, dramatists, historians, sociologists, social activists, etc. to simultaneously evoke, release, and transcend different kinds of personal, political, intuited, and evolving freedoms.

From Free Thinking to Freedom Thinking

As viewers, we are prompted to develop a questioning attitude concerning the circumstantial 'what, why and how' of these variously oblique yet testimonial treatments of freedom, to spark up an imaginary dialogue about the communicability and incommunicability, translatability and untranslatability, and materiality and immateriality of 'freedom' and its manifestation as modern Indian art. We understand this freedom to be present in the new historical, social, and aesthetic ecologies defined by the artists, their markets, their surroundings, their critics, and their students. Yet we are forced to address this freedom cautiously and sensitively, given the incomplete and asymmetric nature of the dialogue and the interpretive challenges presented by each artist's response to the question of and demand for freedom. It is no coincidence, given the focus on non-dualism or interdependence, that the concept of freedom under consideration here invites an interpretation also defined by convergence, for example between its means and its ends. But this does not necessarily clarify or simplify matters. For in any promotion or search for freedom other values may be obscured or sidelined. This predicament may also be true for other, perhaps competing, versions or visions of freedom, especially when these assume greater or lesser prominence in the multiple fields of freedom that are defined by other artworks, other lives, other ideas, other methods, other minds, other words, other goals, or other ideals.

My own understanding of freedom - considered here in respect of India's pre-independence and 'indigenous' artistic cultures - has arisen through an interest in the cross-cultural relevance of the Bengal School and Santiniketan School of Art, as well as the 'Arts of the Adivasi'.[5] This is a phrase that was first put to use by the artist, philosopher and activist Jagdish Swaminathan in the 1980s, in an effort to establish a better understanding of the social and cultural predicament of India's Scheduled Tribes, or Adivasis (literally first 'adi' inhabitants 'vasi'). They were deemed to be custodians of a vision and experience of modern India that was both integral - in terms of its contribution to India's artistic, linguistic, and ethical heritage - yet inherently vulnerable. In attempting to generate complementarity and synergy between non-Adivasi and Adivasi artists and educators, Swaminathan rejuvenated a culture of cross-cultural dialogue and exchange that has since acquired international relevance.

ILLUSTRATION 3 - *Radhacharan Bagchi, Untitled (Santhal Dance) (p. 159)*
This process began in the early to mid twentieth century, when artists like Abanindranath Tagore, Nandalal Bose, Kshitindranath Majumdar, Ramkinkar Baij, Jamini Roy, Deviprasad Roychowdhury, Upendra Maharathi, Ramendranath Chakraborty and others sought to observe, celebrate and picture 'the Adivasi' as a trope of resilience, sustainability, and solidarity. Whilst there are traces of primitivism and romanticism in some of their representations, overall these works are characterised by an intense search: a search for a shared humanity that would contradict the idea that Adivasi culture was totally submerged and beyond repair. That this search was deemed to be liberating - whether for the artist, the Adivasi, or society at large - is suggestive of an emergent ethical and conceptual temperament. In its potential to be translated and shared, this temperament developed into an impulse: to question and therefore refashion the relationship between art, freedom, and modernity at large.

We need to move ahead, therefore, into a domain of 'freedom' thinking that is able to grasp the multiple meanings and usages, as well as the problematic 'humaneness' of freedom: for who or what curates and controls it, and to what ends?

In asking such questions, we should be able to shoulder the responsibility - initially addressed by Tagore - of enabling freedom to remain an open, intercultural, and relatively independent concept, which nourishes the human condition and enhances people's capacity to flourish, individually or collectively. In view of this exhibition, the realm of 'painted', 'created' or 'imagined' freedom - mediated by artists and curators, and interpreted by us (the viewers) - has a capacity to do two things. First, it can inform a new understanding of artistic and political cultures in South Asia, and can do so in manner that can be shared between people whose value systems and sense of freedom may be either quite similar to, or else quite different from, each other especially when we consider our own temporal and spatial distance from the artists' viewpoints. Secondly - by becoming the pivot across which new understandings and dialogues emerge, whether in a direct relation to the art of the past, or in terms of ourselves and our capacity to coexist and to communicate freedom - it can inspire us to keep pushing, pressing, opening the prospects of both independence and interdependence that enable different cultures and meanings of freedom to make sense.

In using the phrase 'prospects of interdependence' we can hint at both the independence and the co-dependence of different types of freedom. In doing so we necessarily delimit, shape, and convey the diverse qualities of these freedoms. We do so less as a way of maintaining their singularity for the sake of it, and more as a means of investing in the qualities of specific freedoms a coherence and a depth of meaning that demonstrates the value of that type of freedom.

This is part of the trade-off that necessarily takes place when we enter into the fields of complexity that animate freedom at large. In searching for specific types or meanings of freedom, and then thinking these through in detail and then describing or communicating them, we both disrupt the overall field and add something to it. In terms of the differently 'painted' cultures of freedom that are presented in the exhibition and that I alluded to above, we need to be aware of this as a process through which the artistic imagining and expression of freedom enabled different parts of the overall field to align with others. In doing so, the artists presented different scales and types of freedom: as compatible, energetic, and meaningful.

ILLUSTRATION 4 - *Kshitindranath Majumdar, Krishna Lila, (p. 145)*
The basic notion of freedom that was at play in the pre-independence phase was later codified into such maxims as 'the personal is political'. The artistic narrative went something like this: *the freedoms inherent in our artistic imagination must be respected, nurtured and communicated to inspire a sense of shared responsibility for ourselves and for our future. Once articulated and absorbed, they can enrich and deepen our consciousness, with the effect of transforming our culture and our society, as well as the future of humanity, which resides in us just as we reside in it.* In aligning modern art overtly to this version of freedom, other scales and dimensions of freedom were invoked. So, in putting freedom 'first', the artists then (and ourselves now) aspired to put the idea of freedom to the test, whether as the amalgamation

of subjective means and shared ends, or as the convergence of India's liberal philosophies, and of mythic and social time, in an era of heightened colonialism and unfreedom.

In putting freedom to the test, they (or we) experimented with it by putting it out there, in front of ourselves and ahead of other ideas. As such, freedom became uppermost in an emergent hierarchy-of-values, which involved diverse value systems and multiple communicative practices, in anticipation that it would synergise efforts towards independence, full personhood, and social equality. It needs to be said that this attitude of putting freedom first pertained directly to the modern artists' sense of themselves as embodiments of India's artistic and philosophical heritage. This is a sense of self (and therefore of self and other) that demonstrated how - via the cultivation of an artistic temperament infused either with a heightened social consciousness or an elevated spiritual mind, or both - freedom could be envisioned and purposefully reproduced. Operating in accordance with other humanistic philosophies, this paideia was termed at the time a 'higher' Swadeshi: with Swa (self) and Deshi (region, country, locality, folk community) combining, not only to develop one's economy and culture along anti-imperial and indigenous lines, but also to inspire one's capacity to communicate, teach, and recreate Swadeshism as freedom.[6]

In short, this alluded to the making of an overtly independent (non-colonial) culture, economy, and polity that would be markedly anti-imperialist in its capacity (a) to combine the pre-colonial and the post-colonial as a new synthesis, and (b) to recalibrate - via the anticipation of national freedom - the asymmetric power-relations in operation between the local, the regional, and the global. It would define the modern artist as the realisation of the capacity of society to transform in conjunction with a whole host of ideas and ideals premised on India's social and intellectual rejuvenation, or its long road to recovery from oppression and unfreedom. The educational and moral leadership role afforded to the fine arts in this process was informed by a long history of freedom thinking: i.e. the idea inherited from the depths of India's devotional, religious and philosophical literature that understood human evolution in terms of the furtherance of freedom, not only from political oppression but also from the inherently negative and constraining aspects of the human condition.

Herein the conscious artistic inclusion of mythological/devotional arts as well as of 'folk' and Adivasi cultures, both at the time and in the exhibition, becomes instructive. For the fine artists were seeking to become fully conscious of their own humanity, their own nationality, as well as of their non-Adivasi identity: i.e. their potential and yet avoidable complicity in a process of neo-colonialism, wherein non-Adivasi cultures would dominate over the 'other within'. So, they self-consciously responded to indigenous (Adivasi) and regional versions and experiences of colonial modernity, and sought to respect and reimagine the prospect that social integration in independent India could and would occur with consent, rather than forcefully via assimilation. It was a self-consciousness that largely contradicted colonialist representations of 'primitive' India in its new capacity to delineate not only a shared nationality but also a shared humanity, for example with the Adivasis, whose collective yet routinely marginalised experiences of social time, as well as of anti-colonial resistance, demanded a prolonged introspection amongst non-Adivasi artists and intellectuals.[7]

The artistic apprehension - in the image of the Adivasi - of lost pre-colonial freedoms gave rise to an intense re-evaluation of, as well as a new kind of respect, for Adivasi aesthetics, customs, beliefs, histories, and migrations. It was an ambiguous discourse because it played with notions of justice and injustice, as well as with the realities and problematics of rebellion, recognition, and renewal. Numerous film-makers, writers, poets, visual artists, journalists, folklorists, anthropologists, sociologists, policy-makers, lawyers, and educators continue to push for this intercultural sense of social inclusion, as means to uphold the nation's commitment to social justice.

In this matrix - at once civilisational and radical, political and universal, individualistic and socialist - the idea of freedom emerges as both the means and the ends of insight, rationality and creativity. This makes freedom a difficult yet necessary feature of further contemplation, as well as of educational and social philosophising. In asking how and why artists paint freedom, this exhibition moves along a route that is seemingly well-charted yet immensely difficult to navigate, given the propensity of some artists to fold themselves and their work into discourses of devotion (Bhakti) and personal liberation (Kaivalya) that alluded to supra-rational and cosmological dimensions of human and planetary existence.

Our Larger Freedom?

In stringing together of a series of reflections on the social, aesthetic and ideational dimensions of freedom, I aim to inspire a reinvigorated dialogue, rather than to chart a new manifesto. What is at stake is our capacity to apprehend and then to learn from the distance that exists between the larger politics of freedom, on the one hand, and, on the other, the individuality that is inherent in artistic expression and in cultural and historical interpretation and praxis.

Importantly, the scope of both of these domains has changed in the century since many of the works in this exhibition were produced or collected. Recourse may be paid, for example, to the work of Isaiah Berlin and subsequent reflections - for example by Partha Chatterjee and Amartya Sen - on his ideas of personal and political freedom and liberty, as well as the capacity of these ideas to inform political philosophy and social science in multiple contexts.[8] Although the now well-hewn concept of our 'larger freedom' had not then been articulated, it was certainly anticipated by radical humanist philosophers in modern India, such as Aurobindo Ghose and Rabindranath Tagore, whose capacity to imagine and operationalise a 'high' Swadeshi provides a good point of re-entry into these spaces.

Their sense of their own and others' individuality was premised upon a vision of 'the total' - a totality that engulfed the whole of India and the whole of humanity - via an understanding and appreciation of the self as a series of relations: of inherent human interconnections (past, present and future), as well as of collapsed, constrained or otherwise conditioned social relations. In this total vision, human individuality could be cultivated at different scales through the development of insights and values - for example of empathy, responsibility, justice, democracy, and solidarity - that enabled the overall vision to become clear and tangible, i.e. lived rather than simply imagined or hoped for. In doing so, they charted a future freedom that would evolve into the 'larger freedom' of independent India and, via the work of organisations such as UNESCO, also into a more universal or global space of human cooperation and artistic exchange celebrating and cultivating human rights, human dignity, and cultural diversity.

ILLUSTRATION 5 - *Kartick Pyne, Untitled, (p. 193)*
Indeed, many exponents of this interplay between consciousness and independence, and between freedom, liberty and responsibility, thought of their own work as more than a silver lining to the horrors of imperialism and related forms of oppression and chauvinism. Whilst this attitude did surface, it was its capacity to inform both national and larger (i.e. more universalistic) spaces of freedom that gave its proponents - for example the fine artists including in this exhibition - the necessary conviction to see themselves and their work less as an addendum to modernity, and more as the pivot across which multiple forms, ideas, beliefs, economies, value systems and knowledge systems could and should coalesce.

This is why and how I would like us to move forward, in view of the artworks displayed in this exhibition: to become responsive to the different ways in which freedom operates in and through their existence, and their communicative and educational potential. To outline the global context of a 'larger freedom' that exists at the cusp of (a) twentieth-century decolonisation, and (b) the 'new' humanism of the twenty-first, is not to marginalise (c) the visual artist whose singular vision or version of freedom is relatively unknown, at least when compared directly with the national and dominant cultures that inhabit the arena of international democracy. Rather it is to humanise that sense of a larger or higher freedom, which largely operates outside of oneself, yet which exists to account for oneself whether as a freedom thinker or as a global citizen, especially as and when one aspires to contribute to the furtherance of human or artistic achievement, less as an individual and more as part of one or more 'freedom' collectives.

To participate in the making of such kinds of collectives is to align oneself within, and to become self-conscious of, both a shared and a differentiated humanity. It is this self-consciousness that characterised the artistic movements towards freedom and independence in India during the early twentieth century. Taking the culture-specific form of stories, relations, aesthetics, values, and environments, these movements have since been sidelined in the history of modern art, largely because they do not conform to Western norms, identities, or beliefs. In view of this sense of indifference, which contradicts the 'human' responsibility to rethink and re-engage these art forms, it remains important to question in more detail how participants within these movements painted freedom, so that this sense of freedom might once again contribute to our own 'larger freedom'. This is no easy task, but it is a task worth pursuing as it can also help us to appreciate the richness and the translatability of the overall message. Then and now, the circumstantial question is fairly similar: where and how does the balance of power, freedom, and expression actually reside? Taken up in this light, the premise of the exhibition - to move within and across a spectrum of artistic engagements with freedom - becomes instructive and interesting. It also becomes a way of reassessing whether and how the cultures of artistic freedom that emerged in the pre-independence era, for example via the ethos of Swadeshi and Swaraj (self-rule, self-determination, self-discipline), may continue to engage and enliven our sense of humanity, and to configure current global as well as human responsibilities.

It will be important to discern the extent to which this reappraisal may be considered a cultural, ethical, political, intellectual, or social challenge. In all likelihood it may be seen as a combination of all of the above. This is because (in my terms) freedom only becomes sensible and meaningful once it's conjunctions with power and responsibility acquire prominence. This then lends itself to another question, as to whether what is being painted or discussed is 'freedom' after all, for it may also and equally be Mukti (as somewhat distinct to Western or Anglo-phonic notions of freedom), or freedom as Wisdom, or art as liberty, or any other configuration.

In all contexts of creativity and expression, particular kinds of artistic and cultural politics do exist. It is important, therefore, to seek to define and understand these politics, whether as distinctive or else as interconnected dynamics, so that whenever we speak of, for, to, or with freedom, or what I would like to call Freedom First, we can properly discern its (variously productive, restricted or troubled) meanings. One of the greatest achievements of freedom is to operate simultaneously as an open and a closed concept - unifying the one with the other, the local with the global, the human with Humanity - whilst somewhat surreptitiously, and without any sense of self-irony, refusing or constraining other kinds of freedom and power.

Freedom in Use

This line of critical thinking is integral both to the creation and curation of all visions of freedom that generate a certain kind of depth as well as a certain patterning. This triangulation of freedom - with power and with responsibility - necessarily enables it to operate at the heart of any conscious search for or expression of freedom-with-power, freedom-with-responsibility, and so on.[9] We are intent on discovering what happens in these spaces of imagination, expression, communication, reception and reflection that are brought into play, whether by modern or by folk artists, as and when they discover and tread the multiple lines that connect freedoms past and freedoms future, or even high (larger; more sustainable) and lower (less valued; ephemeral) freedoms.

Invocations of freedom can take us a long way, for example in the ongoing search for social justice, equality, respect, recognition, rationality, and creativity that many advocates of peace deem to be integral to the betterment of humanity. Through these invocations, the meanings and shapes of freedom - as an idea that can inform attitudes, inspire critique, and define behaviours - become complex. They can rarely be discerned either singularly or overtly as 'freedom'. For they re-combine, re-align, and re-calibrate into new conceptual, linguistic, or artistic forms that may evoke or elaborate freedom, but cannot be expected to encompass the fullness, the totality, or the complexity of freedom at large.

Freedom is and should remain an inherently deep and complex concept, combining the abstract with the embodied, the ideal with the real, the ends with the means. So, how are these qualities to be understood, sustained, and diversified? This is where exhibitions such as this one have a pivotal and immensely timely role to play: to ask, for example, questions about the artistic qualities of freedom that are being expressed, and interpreted and reinterpreted, and to reflect on what may be referred to as the multi-dimensionality of the ever-evolving relationship between art, culture, creativity, decolonisation, and humanity. These are not necessarily easy issues to deal with. Yet, to my mind, they do appear integral to the exhibition, as well as to the functioning of the exhibition in (and as) a contemporary space.

It is a space that aspires to be responsible to the artistic cultures that are being represented, whilst becoming critical of the imperial and post-imperial dynamics that affect the variously historical, social, and educational vacuums that ignore these artists, and what their work might mean to us and to future generations. The problem is that certain versions of independence, and certain hierarchies of value and freedom, became canonised after independence. These privileged certain readings or versions of independence and freedom that were ostensibly the truest, the safest, the most authentic, or the most marketable. They subsumed all of the leading lights of the freedom struggle into a powerful idea - Young India - that could simultaneously know and celebrate itself (especially within the newly independent nation-states and across multiple diasporas) whilst - in an effort to forge a new global role for its contemporary manifestations - keeping its historic exponents at arm's length from 'the West'.

What was lost in all this was a proper dialogue that could impart in the West, and in what is a now the Global North, a nuanced and sustained responsiveness: whether to the problems of identity and difference, of decolonisation and diaspora, or of freedom and social consciousness. It is in these kinds of spaces of contemporary dialogue that one can and indeed should confront what I refer to as the difficulties of navigation: for it is here that both small and large freedoms are routinely compromised and flattened, to the extent that their history and capacity to exert a continued presence is either forgotten or ignored. This is why and how we can attempt to learn from diverse artistic and educational responses to unfreedom and freedom. But the question remains: will our learnings prompt us to engage - collectively, and in a sustainable and fully inclusive manner - the disparate socio-political, ethical (philosophical), and artistic dimensions of freedom?

1 - For a complex yet compelling analysis of both 'dialectical' and 'circumstantial' approaches to freedom, which takes into account their significance in twentieth-century geopolitics, see Richard McKeon, 'Philosophic Differences and the Issues of Freedom', *Ethics*, Volume 61, Number 2, pp. 105-135.

2 - Quoting Creighton Peden, 1978. 'Freedom and Wisdom: The Heart of Tagore', *Journal of Thought*, Volume 13, Number 3, pp. 210-216.

3 - Partha Mitter, 1994. *Art and Nationalism in Colonial India, 1850-1922: Occidental Orientations,* Cambridge: Cambridge University Press.

4 - Daniel Rycroft, 2006. 'Santalism: Reconfiguring 'the Santal' in Indian Art and Politics', *Indian Historical Review,* Volume 33, Number 1, pp. 150-174.

5 - See Jagdish Swaminathan, 1992. 'Art and the Adivasi', *India International Quarterly,* Volume 19, pp. 113-127.

6 - Various authors, 1908. *The Swadeshi Movement: A Symposium,* Madras: G.A. Natesan

7 - See Daniel Rycroft and Sangeeta Dasgupta, eds. 2011. *The Politics of Belonging in India: Becoming Adivasi,* Abingdon: Routledge.

8 - Isaiah Berlin, 1958. *Two Concepts of Liberty: An Inaugural Lecture Delivered Before the University of Oxford on 31 October 1958,* Oxford: Clarendon Press; Partha Chatterjee, 'Berlin, Tagore, and the Dubious Legitimacy of Nationalism', in Bruce Baum and Robert Nichols, eds. *Isaiah Berlin and the Politics of Freedom,* Abingdon: Routledge, pp. 155-183; Amartya Sen, 1990. 'Individual Freedom as a Social Commitment', *New York Review of Books* (14 June), pp. 49-54.

9 - McKeon, 1951, p. 112

Beyond tradition: Hemen Mazumdar and the Triumph of Naturalism

Isabelle Kent

A beautiful nude woman lies sleeping, light dancing off the curves of her body. Although her back is to us, we catch a glimpse of her sleeping face in a mirror. This is the subject of a presentation drawing (p. 312) in ink wash and pen by the Indian artist Hemen Mazumdar (1894-1948). It is one of his few surviving drawings and a masterclass in the modulation of light across a body. The nude with its continuous, sensuous line is instantly recognisable to any student of European painting. It is taken from Diego Velázquez's scandalous the *Toilet of Venus*, better known as the *Rokeby Venus*.

In the early 20th century, the Rokeby Venus was one of the most famous paintings in the British empire. In 1906, following a major public appeal and press coverage, the painting was bought for the National Gallery, London, where it has been prominently displayed ever since. But just eight years later in 1914, 'the Nation's Venus' was slashed by Mary Richardson in the name of women's suffrage. Given its international fame it is no surprise that Mazumdar chose it as the basis for his own work. However, his drawing is no slavish copy. Instead Mazumdar translates the western model into his own visual language, exchanging the nude European Venus for a beautiful Bengali woman and adding familiar and domestic details. The differences are as stark as the similarities. Where Velázquez's model is awake and looking obliquely at the viewer through the mirror, Mazumdar's is peacefully asleep, evoking a sense of romance, tenderness and vulnerability. Also gone are Velázquez's mythological allusions to Venus and the inclusion of a putto. Instead Mazumdar's figure is a living, breathing woman inhabiting a domestic space. These differences remove the ambiguity that exist in Velázquez's painting where the face is indistinct, instead transforming the scene into one of romantic, sensual pleasure.

As a specialist in European early modern painting, I inevitably approach Mazumdar's art with a European visual lexicon. While some may consider this old-fashioned, if any artist can benefit from such a treatment it is Hemen Mazumdar. Born in 1894 in the Kishoreganj District (now Bangladesh), Mazumdar never travelled outside of India. His knowledge of the European masters came predominantly from books, prints and photographs. Despite this he continually framed his own work within the context of western references, transposing the forms of Ingres, Velázquez, Rubens and Titian to his sari-clad women. This conscious and legible referencing and adaptation of past masters is in itself an act of artistic genius associated with the European tradition. It has long been noted that Velázquez himself, in the *Rokeby Venus*, was consciously imitating and reinventing the reclining nudes of Titian. This imitation was by no means a passive act, but rather one that demonstrated the Spaniard's own visual erudition and ability to surpass the masters of the past. Titian in turn looked back to Giorgione, and both were deeply influenced by the classical world, incorporating forms from ancient Greek and Roman sculpture and subjects from literature in an effort to equal and even surpass the great artists of the past. Through his drawing, then, Mazumdar was consciously inserting himself into a lineage of artists that stretched back to Apelles and the ancients, while simultaneously defining his own place within the landscape of Indian art. Such acts demonstrate his belief that mimetic art was not owned by any single culture or tradition but is instead universal.

The complex relationship between Indian artists and the European academic tradition has gained considerable scholarly attention over the past decades.[1] As Partha Mitter noted, the reception of European academic art in the East 'oscillated between enthusiastic acceptance and vehement resistance.'[2] At the point of Mazumdar's entry into the Government College of Art in Calcutta in 1911, the pendulum had swung firmly against the academic realist tradition.

The Government College was at the centre of an effort to reintroduce and, in certain cases, invent an 'Indian-style' of painting.[3] This move was spearheaded by the Englishman and then governor of the school, E. B. Havell, and the artist Abanindranath Tagore, and included a concerted rejection of the European academic curriculum imposed since the founding of the school in the 1850s. Tagore and the Bengal School went so far as to refuse to exhibit the work of academic artists. The abandonment of Academic naturalism infuriated the young Mazumdar, who soon left the college, instead enrolling in Ranada Gupta's Jubilee Academy of Art, an institution more sympathetic to his interests. However, here too he felt the teaching was lacking, and resorted instead to the study of European art through books. It is perhaps relevant that the drawing described above is a mirror image of the *Rokeby Venus*, since Mazumdar may have only known the painting through a reversed print or photograph.

In our society, which has fully embraced modernism as the triumph of early 20th-century art, it is easy to assume that an Indian artist whose work adhered to the European academic tradition was therefore disengaged from the politics of national identity and independence. For Mazumdar this could not be further from the truth. As Jomabhoy has noted, he saw his academic naturalism as part of the effort to remove distinction between the coloniser and the colonised, and to express universal themes including love, desire and death. In his 1929 essay 'The Making of a Picture', he writes that, despite visual difference between painters, there is 'a certain unity or community of spirit in the things that really matter in the pictures of all masters, past and present.'[5] This 'stamp of genius', as he called it, is not the privilege of one people or another but exists throughout time and space.
Mazumdar wrote numerous scathing critiques of the sentimentality of Tagore's Bengal School, which he believed looked nostalgically backward, rather than forging a modern scientific visual language based on the merits of form, chiaroscuro and proportion. In 1919 he founded the Indian Academy of Art alongside his friends Atul Bose and the great Jamini Roy (who, at the time, was a supporter of naturalism) with the aim of counteracting the growing prominence of the Bengal School. However, Mazumdar was not simply a

reactionary or polemicist. The Indian Academy created a space for all Indian artists, not just those of the academic tradition, to exhibit, publicise and discuss their work, and in 1929 he founded the journal Shilpi as a 'arena for free discussion and exchange of thoughts relative to the fine arts – Oriental and Occidental, Ancient and Modern'.[6]

Mazumdar arguments in favour of naturalism were not limited to the written word. In a rare still life, *A Dry Feast (fig. 1)*, he plays with the ability of naturalistic art to trick the eye. The painting depicts a chaotic studio where four cats have knocked over a half-finished painting of seafood and are attempting to eat the two-dimensional prawns depicted within. One cat's tail is covered in red paint and another is pawing at a painted fish-head as if expecting it to roll. There are echoes of Jean-Baptiste Siméon Chardin's *The Ray*, which Mazumdar may well have seen in reproduction. The delightful subject is surely a witty take on the famous story of Zeuxis and Parrhasius of Ephesus. Pliny in his *Natural History* tells of a contest between the two great painters to determine who is the most skillful. Zeuxis' painting depicts a bunch of grapes so realistic that birds fly down from the trees to try and eat them. He then turns to Parrhasius, whose painting is hidden behind a curtain. Zeuxis attempts to pull back the curtain, only to discover that the curtain itself is painted. From the Renaissance onwards this anecdote was used as an argument for the supremacy of naturalism. While playful, Mazumdar's innovative painting also speaks to his sincere commitment to the art of academic naturalism.

In the decade after graduating from Jubilee Academy, Mazumdar established a new genre of painting in India that re-envisioned the age-old theme of the sensual female figure. His voyeuristic paintings of elite Bengali women, elegantly posed and often clad in his signature 'wet sari' effect were highly sought after by the middle classes of Calcutta and beyond. In these paintings Mazumdar channelled the ancient Greek sculptural models that he would have seen in books and perhaps in plaster casts. He also looked to masterpieces by the French neo-Classical painter, Jean-Auguste-Dominique Ingres, emulating the elongated nude back of the *Valpinçon Bather* in his numerous paintings of women seen from behind. However, these are not the impersonal classicised figures churned out by so many late 19th-century European artists. Instead, his semi-nude figures are simultaneously tangible, real Bengali women while also being universal images of sensual, romantic beauty.

A particularly poignant image is *In Expectation (pp. 302-303)*. It depicts an upper-class woman dressed in a luxurious yellow sari and leaning against the doorframe of her home. This would have been a common enough sight in the wealthy districts of Calcutta as young wives rarely stepped out of their homes, instead waiting by the door for their husbands. The large scale of the painting (it measures 114 x 75.5 cm) and close focus creates a strong sense of immediacy, with the door becoming an illusory picture frame with her hand breaking the surface of the space. Such a effect is reminiscent of *Two Women at a Window* by the Spanish master Bartolomé Esteban Murillo, where he creates a fictive window with a girl leaning on the frame and another laughing at us. This device was also common in the paintings of Dutch seventeenth-century masters such as Gerrit Dou, but Murillo, like Mazumdar, heightens the intimacy by painting the figures close to life size. However, where Murillo's girls are jovial and provocative, Mazumdar's picture evokes the loneliness and longings of a young Bengali wife.

Mazumdar's preoccupation with capturing the universal themes of the human condition led him to utilise the symbolism of the European academic tradition. In the Goal (fig. 2) he depicts a beautiful woman seated on a tomb-like bench and pondering a skull. Beside her is a dying rose, petals strewn over the floor. With its overt symbolism the painting is a thinly veiled allegory for death, connecting to the popular tradition of Vanitas painting that flourished from the seventeenth century onwards. It is also reminiscent of the many depictions of the Penitent Magdalene praying with a skull in hand. Mazumdar removes any Christian references, instead choosing a universal narrative, that of a woman mourning a lost love. Particularly intriguing is the inclusion of a graceful sculpture of a dancing goddess. While Mazumdar has emphasised the old masters in the painting's subject matter, his inclusion of the beautiful nude sculpture is a reminder than naturalism isn't the preserve of the European academic tradition.

At the heart of his practice is the use of the life model. According to an essay in the 1921 edition of *Indian Academy of Art*, the development of his 'wet sari effect' took 'several months labour with his models at his Calcutta studio'.[7] He continued to utilise the model, often his beloved wife, throughout his career.[8] We can see his skill in drawing from the model in a rare sheet, *Memories terrible of a nude woman* (fig. 3), which includes some seven sketches in ink and wash of a women in various poses. However, his use of a model was not merely a means to hone his skills and achieve correct proportion. In his 1929 essay, Mazumdar outlines the importance of finding the perfect model if the artist will achieve the ultimate goal of a universal truth. First the artist must picture in their mind the ideal form of the figure they wish to convey - he uses the example of a beggar. Once they have completed a sketch of this, they must go and search for an individual who comes close to the mental image. The artist must be diligent in their search, as not any beggar will do. In fact, the individual chosen may not even be a beggar but simply have an essence of 'beggarliness' about them. Such diligence pays off as 'the artist's beggar will make you realize at once what grim poverty is in all its nakedness.'

In a small Untitled, oil sketch (fig. 4), Mazumdar outlines the transformative power of painting from the model. The scene is that of an artist's studio. A partially nude model holds a contrapposto pose with an arm raised covering her face and knee bent resting on a box. The artist's pallet rests on a stool in the fore ground, behind which is a large unfinished canvas and a small preparatory sketch. The trope of the artist at work in the studio is common in European painting, Johannes Vermeer's *The Art of Painting* being perhaps the most famous example. Yet here Mazumdar removes the artist all together, leaving the viewer to stand in their place as if we are the ones to have laid down the palette. This highly innovative composition allows for a critical comparison between the model and the canvas and sketch. Most striking is the halo included in the large canvas. In the sketch too the shadowy figure is standing on a mound of some sort – perhaps it depicts the birth of Venus? Regardless of the exact subject, the painted figure is distinctly different from the flesh and blood model posed in the studio; it is somehow transcendent, more ethereal and disconnected from the mundanity of a dingy, dimly lit room. Mazumdar then is demonstrating in oils what he described with such passion in his essay, that through the depiction of a real individual, the artist can capture something universal, in this case the sensual elegance of womankind as opposed to the beauty of a single woman.

After his death Mazumdar and his academic style fell out of favour, and his name was largely forgotten until the 1990s. However, his search for universality through mimetic art points to the need to move beyond tightly sealed, nationalist histories of art. Modernism never completely did away with the representation of the human body, and the current resurgence of figurative painting in contemporary art is perhaps a vindication of Mazumdar's goals. By taking that most ancient of artistic subjects, the female nude, and reinterpreting it, Mazumdar both asserted the 'Indianness' of his art while also situating himself in a borderless landscape of naturalist painting.

Fig. 1
H. Mazumdar
Untitled (A Dry Feast),
Watercolour on paper pasted on board
39,4×57,7 cm

Fig. 2
H. Mazumdar
The Goal
Oil on canvas
71,8x50,2 cm

Fig. 4
H. Mazumdar
Untitled
Oil on canvas
33,3x43,2 cm

Fig. 3
H. Mazumdar
Memories terrible of a nude woman
Ink on paper
23x19 cm

1 - See Partha Mitter, *Art and Nationalism in Colonial India:* 1850-1922, (Cambridge University Press, Cambridge, 1994) and Geeta Kapur 'A Stake in Modernity: A Brief History of Modern Indian Art', in *Art and Social Change: Contemporary Art in Asia and the Pacific*, ed. Caroline Turner (Pandanus Books, Canberra, 2005), pp. 146-63.

2 - Mitter 1994, p. 4.

3 - Mitter 1994, pp. 279-83

4 - Zehra Jumabhoy, 'The Look of Love: Desire and the National Imagination', in *Hemen Mazumdar: The Last Romantic*, ed. Catherine Corsini and Nirmalya Kumar (Singapore, 2019), p. 116.

5 - Hemendranath Mazumdar, 'The Making of a Painting', *Shilpi: An Illustrated Journal of the Fine Arts*, Calcutta, 1929. Reprinted in *Hemen Mazumdar: The Last Romantic*, ed. Catherine Corsini and Nirmalya Kumar (Singapore, 2019), p. 13.

6 - Quoted in Partha Mitter, *The Triumph of Modernism: India's artists and the avant-garde, 1922-1947*, p. 133

7 - Quoted in Pathar Mitter, 'Hemendranath and the Vexed Question of the Wet Sari Effect', in *Hemen Mazumdar*: The Last Romantic, ed. Catherine Corsini and Nirmalya Kumar (Singapore, 2019), p. 95

8 - Guha-Thakurta 1992, p. 321.

Art Authentication and The Bengal School

Nirmalya Kumar
Lee Kong Chian Professor of Marketing, Singapore Management University

All too often, Indian art observers see paintings with their ears, rather than their eyes. Not having developed a deep well of visual vocabulary, and therefore, unable to trust their eyes, the viewers search their memory for what have they heard about this artist, what have they been told about the reputation and reliability of the source, and the many whispered conspiracy theories related to the ubiquity of fakes in Indian art. Perhaps, it is the natural response if one is not schooled on the subject and lacks confidence in their ability to judge, but wishes to project an appearance of being knowledgeable.

As someone, who has spent more than three decades collecting art, a surprising revelation was that prevailing best practices do not allow for a foolproof method of establishing the authenticity of an artwork. Estimates vary, but some claim that as much as a tenth to a third of all the artworks circulating are forgeries.[1] This seems rather high, and one assumes that it relates to works by deceased artists. However, it implies that to some extent we are all taking a leap of faith when attributing authorship of an artwork to an artist, especially for deceased artists. Yet, this does not mean that we cannot be more or less confident about any particular artwork's attribution. Our conviction on authenticity can range from none to almost certain.

We gain confidence about the authorship of an artwork through a triangulation of methods: provenance, expert eye or stylistic connoisseurship, and technical analysis. Each of these three approaches are discussed in turn, especially noting their weaknesses in order to support the central thesis, that ultimately, there is always some leap of faith involved in establishing authenticity. I conclude with some observations on my own approach to the problem of "fakes" as a collector of the Bengal School of Art. However, first, we must consider what a "fake" is.

Imitations, Misattributions, Fakes, and Forgeries

With the old masters like Canaletto or Rubens, it was all about distinguishing the "hand" of the master from those of the assistants. The advent of the camera meant that a great painter does not necessarily make for a great artist, as it is about having a new, unique or a big idea. As Marcel Duchamp pronounced, 'it is artist's choice, not hand that determines a genuine work'. Duchamp's most famous creation was after all an upside-down, locally sourced, mass-produced, porcelain urinal called Fountain in 1917. Following this, anything signed by an artist is considered "genuine" in the art world, because one is buying the mind of the artist, not the hand. Thus, authorship of an artwork is established by artist choice or selection. One artist supposedly quipped: 'After I come up with the idea, do I have to paint it too?'. In this vein, Sol LeWitt (1928-2007) went as far as to state that the idea itself is the work of art. After which, he claimed, one may delegate the actual production to assistants or simply never make it all. The material existence of the artwork was irrelevant, and a set of directions on how to produce the artwork was sufficient for LeWitt. Studios, and the use of assistants, have been around for a long time. Between 1508 and 1512, Michelangelo had help painting the backgrounds of the Sistine Chapel ceilings. The increasing popularity of large-scale site installations, technologically complex works, and multimedia art have made the use of assistants even more common. Consequently, most successful contemporary artists like Anish Kapoor, Damien Hirst and Takashi Murakami have a studio to help them execute works. Jeff Koons admitted to having 150 assistants, arguing "if I had to be doing this myself, I wouldn't even be able to finish one painting a year."[2] Andy Warhol, whose output exceeds 100,000 works, is considered to have perfected the "factory" approach of churning out large number of works.

The precursor of this method in Indian art was Jamini Roy (1887-1972), whose two assistants (son Potol babu and Manindra Chatterjee) sometimes filled in the colour or added the embellishments after he painted the primary lines.[3] Both assistants of Jamini were devoted to him and never painted the primary lines. But because this practice was rare in Indian art at that time, it led to the erroneous conclusion that the assistants had more substantial roles in the making of Jamini artworks and that Jamini maintained a studio. As Howard Hodgkin once jibed about Jamini Roy, "you could have the image in any size: small, medium, or large."[4]

The words fake and forgery, especially in the Indian art world, are bandied about without precise definitions. This is about more than simply semantics because of the detrimental impact it has on collectors and the art market. To understand the differences between imitations, misattributions, fakes, and forgeries, one needs to uncover the intent to deceive, as well as the extent of physical "creation" involved, ranging from a small modification to an existing item or its provenance, to making something deceptive from scratch. Based on this, the following classification in Figure 1 is proposed.

Figure 1: Taxonomy of Potentially Misleading Artworks

		Extent of Creation Involved	
		NONE TO LIMITED	SUBSTANTIAL
Intention to Deceive	NO	Scholarly Misattribution	Imitations
	YES	Fakes	Forgeries

At the most innocent level are imitations - copying of works with no intention to deceive. As part of their training and development, all budding artists attempt to reproduce iconic works of famous artists. One must master the past before seeking to present one's own unique contribution and style. When Michelangelo was young, collectors preferred classical antiquities to contemporary sculptures. Michelangelo sculpted a statue of Sleeping Eros, which was sold after aging to a Cardinal in Rome. It is still unclear if Michelangelo intended it as a forgery, or simply as an imitation that was subsequently aged by the dealer who sold it.

Once the forgery was discovered, the furious Cardinal returned the statue to the dealer for a refund. Yet, impressed by the 21-year old's talent, the Cardinal invited Michelangelo under his patronage to Rome. The dealer managed to resell the sculpture at a lower price. Once Michelangelo's reputation soared, subsequent resales of the sculpture fetched even higher prices than the original sale to the Cardinal. Florentine artists in the 15th century were expected to imitate classical sculptures as part of their training. Even today, Chinese art students are encouraged to copy historical masterpieces during their studies.

In the context of the Bengal School, a quick check of Instagram will reveal that Jamini is the most imitated artist. Perhaps it is because his style seems so deceptively simple. The ubiquity of these imitations, combined with futility of attempting to reproduce Jamini's quintessential strokes and fluidity, allows observers to easily identify them as imitations. It is important to note here that most Jamini imitations are watercolour, gouache, or tempera on paper, which in contrast to oil on canvas are much harder to rework when mistakes happen. Unlike other artists whose imitations may be challenging for even the expert eye to discern, this leads to the inaccurate conclusion that there are many Jamini "fakes".

Further along the spectrum are misattributions, when the work of one artist is mistakenly presented as being that of another. The big difference between misattributions versus imitations and forgeries is that there is no physical creation involved. Misattributions can be either honest errors in scholarship or done with an intention to deceive. The latter are fakes, which will be addressed next. When further scholarship results in a new attribution, the valuation can change dramatically in either direction.

Cardsharps, a painting attributed to a "follower of Caravaggio" was sold by Sotheby's for £42,000 in 2014. The buyer, himself a Caravaggio scholar, declared it to be by the hand of Caravaggio (1571-1610) himself. Disagreements between experts are still raging, but if accepted as a work of the master himself, the valuation would soar to over £10 million. Similarly, in the mid-1980s, a painting of the battle at Seringapatam attributed to William Daniell (1769-1837) was offered for sale at Christie's. It was withdrawn after the Turner experts at Tate Britain correctly attributed it to Joseph Mallord William Turner (1775-1851). Tate subsequently acquired it for their permanent collection and included it in their 2020-21 exhibition, Turner and the Modern World.

Revisions and debates on authorship are a frequent occurrence in the world of old masters. In 1957, the Duke of Devonshire in lieu of tax offered one of his three Rembrandts to the UK government. One of them - Old Man in Armchair was selected to enter the National Gallery collection. In 1968, then leading Rembrandt expert, Horst Gerson, declared it to be the work of a follower, and left it out of the catalogue raisonné. In agreement, the National Gallery included the work in their 2010 exhibition on "fakes and mistakes". But, in 2014, Professor Van de Wetering, director of Rembrandt Research Project, declared it an important painting from an experimentation phase in 1651, when the artist had decided to start all over again and reinvent how he painted (the later "rough manner"). However, National Gallery shrugged and left it out of their 2014-15 exhibition entitled, Rembrandt: The Late Works.

When misattributions are deliberately made with an intention to deceive and to raise the value of an artwork, we are in the domain of fakes. Fakes attempt to deceive, either by misrepresenting the artwork by attributing to another artist or by altering an item. This includes knowingly making false verbal claims that the artwork is by someone other than the actual artist, altering the work for example, by adding a signature or "completing" the work, or creating fabricated provenance papers. Unlike forgeries, the act of creating the work is limited here, but the intention to deceive is paramount.

In Indian art, Sunayani Devi (1875-1962) was an artist who never pursued painting with the expectation of selling her artworks. As a result, as far as we know, she never signed her paintings. The unsigned Sunayani Devi paintings included in the Painting Freedom exhibition were acquired directly from her grandson. Once when I mentioned to her grandson that I had seen a Sunayani Devi painting that incorporated her signature at a gallery, he raised his eyebrows and remarked, "what did her signature look like?"

Jamini Roy sold his artworks mostly out of his Calcutta home, which also doubled as his studio. The house was packed with his unsigned artworks, which he usually autographed when handing them over to the buyer. When potential buyers visited his studio and expressed interest in acquiring a particular type of work that was not in the front studio, Jamini would instruct one of his two assistants in Bengali to fetch such a work from the backroom. If the buyer was satisfied with the artwork in the assistant's possession, Jamini would then sign it and hand it over. This led to rumours that Jamini was signing his assistants' artwork and passing them off as his own. When Jamini died, his studio contained many unsigned paintings. The story goes that some of his descendants thought that the artworks would be more valuable signed, and hence attempted to develop a stencil of his signature that could be applied to these unsigned works. The popularity among Indian art students to copy his works, the ease of spotting them, and Jamini's practice of executing the same image repeatedly, and signing on delivery, have all riddled the market with stories of Jamini fakes.

Forgeries are artworks specifically created to pass off as the real thing. As elaborated in the following sections, using a combination of provenance, expert eye, and technical analysis, one attempts to weed out these forgeries from the real thing. However, it is not a fool proof process. The greater the proficiency of the forger, the less likely the artwork is to be discovered as a forgery. Consequently, in a candid moment, one director of the Metropolitan Museum of Art in New York admitted that he had no idea how many fakes were hanging at the Met.

It is frustrating to be a collector of Bengal School art because prevailing artist practices were not conducive to detecting forgeries. Hemendranath Mazumdar and Jamini Roy repeatedly executed, with relatively minor modifications, the same image. They were following a long Indian tradition (miniatures, Kalighat School, Early Bengal Oils) of copying themselves over time. Jamini felt that this made his art less elitist and more accessible for the middle classes. Furthermore, as is clear from the Painting Freedom exhibition, with the exception of Rabindranath Tagore (1861-1941), Bengal School artists seldom dated their works.

More generally, keeping records was not a practice among Indian artists. Relatively few, like Jogen Chowdhury (born 1939) and Ganesh Pyne (1937-2013), were somewhat meticulous in maintaining records of the artworks they produced. Moreover, lack of a catalogue raisonné and in-depth scholarship on individual artists of Bengal School, further enhances the general confusion vis-à-vis authenticity. Critical art history studies and art criticism are still nascent in India. As anecdotal evidence, I am unable to recall a negative review of an art exhibition in any Indian publication. It is simply unimaginable that a scathing review, of the type that the late Brian Sewell would frequently do of Damien Hirst or Tracey Emin exhibitions, would be published for a famous Indian artist.

Despite all of the above, my controversial contention is that the proportion of forgeries in Indian art is probably less than those prevailing in Western art. Why? First, unlike Western art, where prices above US$50 million for an individual work are not rare anymore, Indian art prices are relatively low. The most expensive Indian painting sold at an auction has been for about five million dollars. US$ three million is the entry point for the five most expensive Indian paintings ever sold at auctions. At the more reasonable end, enough Jamini Roy artworks with excellent provenance can be acquired for between US$10-20 thousand. In other words, the incentive for great artists to give up their own careers, and instead, pursue a life of anonymity and criminality by forging masters is much lower in Indian art.

Second, tens of thousands of art students graduate from China and especially, Western nations annually. Any list of the top 100 art schools in the world will be overwhelmed by North American, Western European, and Chinese universities with some representation from Australian, Korean, and Latin American schools. But, Indian art institutions are absent. In other words, besides the demand factor of prices, the supply of highly accomplished (capable of making great forgeries) Indian students graduating from leading institutions is limited.

Finally, even a modestly above average contemporary Indian artist can command asking prices that rival those comparable to the Jamini Roy prices noted above. This leads one to ask: Who are these mysterious supremely talented people working somewhere in Kolkata or Shantiniketan who can fake Jaminis, Hemens, and Tagores so easily but yet do not wish to pursue their own independent careers? Based on what one observes for the two artists, Hemen and Jamini, that I have followed closely, the quality of "forgeries" is poor and easily exposed. In general, it is an exceptional forger who has the talent to copy originals or create artworks in a style that can rival that of a famous master.

The best forgers are highly accomplished artists themselves, whose own career never took off. Sometimes their motivation is to expose the art world with their forgeries. It is a kind of revenge against the connoisseurs for not recognizing the forger's talent. After being caught, they may even find a reasonable career selling "original reproductions". As Robert Driessen, who admitted to producing thousands of forged oil paintings and sculptures, claims on his website: "Original reproductions of other artists' work, but still specialising in Giacometti bronze statues and pictures." All of his work is signed R. Driessen, and are "perfect copies of the work of the world's best and most famous artists."

The best defense against being duped by forgeries is a combination of provenance, the expert eye of a connoisseur, and extensive technical analysis. To engage in this is both time consuming and costly. It can be comprehensively pursued only for the more expensive artworks. This implies that forgeries of relatively modest priced artworks are more likely to escape detection because these works are unlikely to be subjected to a comprehensive scrutiny. However, this is counter-balanced by the fact that the lower prices will not attract the best forgers and this should make it easier to uncover the forgeries.

Provenance

Provenance is establishing a direct link from the artist's studio to the artwork's present location, or the documented ownership history. Often, the most compelling is an acceptance by living artists, standing in front of their work and acknowledging it as their own. What could be more unambiguous than this? While this is about as good as it gets in the art authentication world, there are potential problems here too.

Allegedly, several famous artists have supposedly passed off the works of their students as their own. However, one must be skeptical of these claims and ask the following two questions. First, is there any documentation to say that the master signed the assistant's work? Second, is there a single case of an assistant in Indian art complaining that the master passed her work off as his own? More importantly, we must remember that this is not an issue if we accept the "artist selection" argument set out above. While, the exploitation of students is a legitimate concern, it is tangential to the problem of authorship. Once signed by the artist and acknowledged as their work, it is the artist's work – period. However, an historian, collector, or viewer one may judge such a work, and its importance differently from those that are considered as being entirely of the master's own hand. Recognizing this, Rubens (1577-1640) priced paintings out of his studio differentially based on whether it was: (1) entirely his work; (2) his work with help of assistants; (3)

mostly the assistants' effort with minor improving flourishes by him; or (4) wholly the assistants' output. These distinctions have now collapsed with artists like Damien Hirst and, for example, his "factory manufactured" spot paintings.[7]

The more intriguing issue is when living artists declare works that reappear at auctions and galleries as not being their own. In Indian art, this has happened more than once. To avoid the risk of litigation, I will avoid identifying the artists but they are marquee names among Indian modern masters. Particularly noteworthy is the example of an artist who walked into a gallery, where several of his works were on display, and declared all of them as forgeries. Why would an artist deny authorship? Greed and legacy seem to be the two most frequent drivers.

As noted previously, Indian modern artists did not command high prices relative to international artists, and often, not even what was needed to support a comfortable lifestyle. When Indian art prices suddenly spiked during the first decade of this century, artists observed paintings that they had sold twenty years ago for perhaps INR10,000, reappearing on the secondary market at hundred, and sometimes, even at thousand times the primary sale price. Since there are no resale rights (artist royalties on secondary sales) in India, many artists felt shortchanged.

The greed factor has also led Western artists, who had seen prices of their creations skyrocket during their lifetime, into disavowing early works. But, some artists have also been motivated by concerns about their reputation. As artists develop over their careers, for example Gerhard Richter (born 1932), the materials employed, the forms favoured, and the signature style identifying them can transform dramatically. Sometimes, artists may not wish to be associated with their earlier body of work, considering them detrimental to their artistic status and legacy. Beyond simply denying that it is their work, artists may also muddy the waters by disowning certain works. Certain civil law jurisdictions (e.g. France, Germany and Italy) actually give artists and writers the right to 'withdraw' or take their name off earlier works they no longer want to be associated with, provided they pick up the damages that such actions cause. While this is not possible under United Kingdom or United States law, informal norms may differ in practice. Richard Prince (born 1949), who found fame in the 1980s, claimed to have destroyed more than 500 of his works from the 1970s.[8] This still left many of his works from this era in important museum and private collections. Most museums, gallerists, and auction houses tend to respect the wishes of living artists. As a result, New York's Guggenheim Museum in their retrospective of Richard Prince dated the artist's career from 1980. Major gallerists do not sell the Prince work from the 1970s and museums generally do not include them in exhibitions. To give Richard Prince credit, he does not claim these early works are not his, rather his argument is that he is rescinding approval of them as they do not represent his artistic vision anymore. If we accept that it is artist selection, not hand, which determines authenticity, then the early works are not Richard Prince's anymore! Yet, there are collectors and gallerists who are now stuck with them. After the artist's death, I suspect all bets are off, but these early pieces are unlikely to ever command the prices of later "authorized" works.

In contrast, Giorgio de Chirico (1888-1978) backdated some of his works made in the 1940s by more than twenty years to when his work was more highly sought and critically acclaimed. During de Chirico's metaphysical period (1911 to 1917), his dreamlike paintings were unlike anything his then contemporaries Matisse and Picasso were doing, or the impressionists before them. However, in 1918, after seeing Titian's Sacred and Profane Love, he turned his back on avant-garde, and instead sought inspiration from the old masters. Not finding the same success of his early years, de Chirico repeated or "re-elaborated" many of his paintings from the metaphysical period in his later decades.

For deceased artists, provenance is viewed as crucial for establishing authenticity. Yet, for older works, often there are gaps in ownership history. These have to be partially supplemented by other documentation such as having been in a famous collection, attached auction or gallery labels, and evidence of being included in exhibitions or publications. While none of these is infallible, a "fake" painting that has been exposed to many would be more likely to have garnered objections along the way. Furthermore, it is reasonable to assume that each institution, curator, and writer that handled the painting engaged in some due diligence.

A solid provenance can compensate for, and even overcome, the objections of experts. However, one must be wary, as sometimes, as the saying goes, the thicker the file supporting the authentication of a work, the more likely it is to be fake. Consider the forger, John Myatt, who painted 200 artworks between 1986 and 1995 in the style of nine modern masters including Braque, Matisse, and Giacometti.[9] The fake paintings were rather unremarkable, having been made with K-Y Jelly and a household emulsion paint that had not been invented until ten years after the alleged dates of the paintings. No technical analysis was conducted and some experts muted their initial reservations because of the detailed fake provenance papers that supported each painting.

The fabricated provenances were by Myatt's patron, John Drewe, who created ownership history from dead and fictitious persons, forged correspondence on official letterheads from respectable institutions like Institute of Contemporary Art London, faked catalogues of defunct but previously prestigious galleries, as well as authentication certificates from a non-existent firm called Art Research Associates. Based on this documentation, Sotheby's sold 14 of Myatt's forgeries. The relative importance of the provenance versus the forged artworks can be demonstrated by the fact that Myatt received only US$165,000 for the 200 works he created. The value creation was in constructing the fake provenances.

In evaluating provenance, the last owner is critical. It is preferable to buy works where the last owner is still alive. When the last owner is deceased then due diligence on the painting becomes more challenging. If, for example, the claim is that the particular artwork was from Lady Ranu Mookerjee's collection (a renowned Bengal School art patron), it leads to a dead end since she died more than two decades ago. Overtime, this issue afflicts even works that were legitimately acquired during the lifetime of the last owner. For example, as mentioned earlier, the Sunayani Devi paintings featured in this book were acquired while her grandson and his wife were alive. However, they both passed away over the past decade and all that remains is a note from one of them. Whereas, if either was alive, anyone so desiring so could have interviewed them to enquire about these paintings.

In contrast, the zamindar and his son, whose home the Hemen Mazumdar artworks originate from are alive. Hemen maintained a studio there in the late 1930s after Hemen's great patron, the Maharaja of Patiala, died. Yet, all this confirms is the zamindar's claim that Hemen painted them. Over the years, someone could have substituted the genuine artworks with copies. Similarly, this can be true for any artworks in this exhibition that were sourced directly from the artist (e.g., Karthik Pyne), their families (e.g., children of Atul Bose, Mukul De, and Quamrul Hasan, or spouse of Gopal Ghose), close associates (e.g., Debi Prasad Roy Chowdhury's personal assistant, Somnath Hore's caster), or even famous collections (e.g., Rabindranath Tagore from Elmhirst collection). None of us were there when these artworks were originally created and neither have we lived with them since then. As a result, while establishing the source credibility and provenance is important, the corroboration that comes from the judgment of an expert is still required.

Connoisseurship and Expert Eye

Connoisseurship, the admittedly fallible eye of an expert, is critical in rendering a judgement. To arrive at a verdict on genuineness, the expert stitches together provenance, sometimes technical analysis, and most importantly, what they "see" with their experienced eye. To be recognized as an expert, one must have studied the artist for years, written papers, organized exhibitions, and depending on the output of the artist, personally examined dozens, maybe even hundreds of works. This requires complete immersion into the life and career of a single artist.

In the western art world, the norm is for experts to specialise in a single artist. Unfortunately, such experts are not readily available for the Bengal School. In India, all too often, one encounters authenticators who are experts in, and authenticate multiple artists. In the absence of credible authenticators, descendants get into this "business" with limited discerning power and ample conflict of interest. Some descendants even start acquiring works from the market, to benefit from the arbitrage on resale, when presented as works from their inherited collection.

Over the years, connoisseurship in general, and number of experts specifically, have declined. As art schools have become more enamored by the political and social implications of art, conceptual art, and the historical movements in art, the focus placed on deeply analyzing specific artists and copying masterpieces has wilted. Consequently, in recent times, fewer students are graduating with the technical skills to become authenticators.

Furthermore, the expertise traditionally available in prestigious auction houses has been strained by the increased volume of works and diversity of artists handled annually. Typically, the South Asian art department at Christie's or Sotheby's will have four to six employees. So, how much expertise can there be on individual artists? In addition, they have greater financial demands, having become publicly listed companies, sometimes before being taken private again. An inherent conflict of interest arises from having to deliver higher sales each year. Despite this, the auction houses mentioned have been around for more than two centuries. Their success is partly because they have invested in building credible reputations by taking the long-term perspective. Any errors are less due to malicious intent on part of the employees, but more a result of operating under significant financial and time pressures.

For the purposes of authentication, it is important to distinguish between types of artists. For a trained artist with a distinctive stroke and a style honed over a lifetime, like Jamini Roy or Hemen Mazumdar, producing a fake is challenging. Thus, an expert's eye is a reliable judge. As one leading Indian art gallery owner once remarked: "Jamini is impossible to fake." On the other hand, for an untrained artist with a continuously experimenting and evolving short career, like Rabindranath Tagore, it is difficult for the connoisseur to give a definitive judgment. Instead, one needs to place greater reliance on provenance and technical analysis.

Despite, having encountered Rabindranath Tagore's art for thirty years, I am still unable to discern the genuine works. But, I have observed that all of his portraits tend to have a similar nose, which is what I look for. Apparently, he was just not enough of a skilled artist to vary this particular feature. This method of looking is called the Morellian analysis, which argues that examining the smallest details such as ears, fingers, or nostrils helps provide clues on the authorship because artists unconsciously leave a "fingerprint" of themselves.[10] They tend to execute some small detail similarly and idiosyncratically across their works. The educated eye learns to look for that in order to spot a particular master's work. However, this method assumes that artists do not change, experiment, do poorer quality works with less effort expended, or have an off day. Furthermore, a sophisticated forger may also have spotted this. Therein lies the limitation of Morellian analysis, and in general, the expert eye.

For the Painting Freedom exhibition, we had two experts - Caterina Corni on Hemen Mazumdar and Sona Datta on Jamini Roy - who are considered the best in the world for these two artists. What these experts have achieved through their obsessive engagement with the artist is an ability to look forensically at an artwork by the master in question. They combine confidence in their judgment with a humility to know that authentication is not an exact science. When experts offer opinions, both type 1 (false positive) and type 2 (false negative) errors are possible. This is why experts disagree, and it helps explain the earlier examples of attribution and reattribution of the Caravaggio and Rembrandt works. Or, the current controversy between experts on whether the Salvator Mundi is the work of Leonardo da Vinci.[11]

To demonstrate the value of an "expert eye" let us consider Hemen Mazumdar. As noted earlier, Hemen repeatedly painted the same image. His more popular works are available in different sizes and mediums such as pen and ink, watercolour on paper, and oil on canvas. The challenge for the expert eye is to account for the evolution of the artist. The earlier versions of Hemen's oil paintings applied layers of paint, which resulted in a deeper and a more luminous look. Later versions were typically painted with less detailed backgrounds and fewer layers of paint. Such simplification is not unusual for artists. Consider the late Turners that portended the Impressionists. Despite painting the same composition, there can be significant differences discernable by the expert between Hemen's two genuine versions, one painted in 1920 and the other in1940. The expert accounts for artist progression in discerning the genuine versus the imitation or forgery.

Exhibits A and B present two versions of "Finishing Touch" attributed to Hemen Mazumdar. Clearly, the signature is more elaborate in version B, while hard to discern in version A. However, the presence of a genuine signature does not make for a watertight case. At the end of his life, Dali was signing blank pieces of paper on his hospital bed. Rather, let us compare versions A and B with the help of our 'Hemen' expert, Caterina Corni. She looked at the two paintings forensically and made the following five observations:

1. In the exhibit B, Hemen Mazumdar created the voluptuousness of the figure through the colour of the skin, which consequently assumes a powerfully expressive value. Soft lines and elegant volumes emerge through the shifting transitions of colour in the figure's complexion, making it seem alive and breathing.
2. In the exhibit A, we can see an elaborated but extremely rigid hairdo which is completely different from exhibit B, where the hair quality is much superior in terms of colours as well as shape. This, and the previous point, contribute to give to the female figure an extraordinary intensity and a balanced harmony of volumes in exhibit B, unlike exhibit A.
3. Earrings are a leitmotif in Hemen's paintings. In exhibit B, the earring is depicted in an elaborate and luminous way, making it stand out in a dramatic contrast against the dark background. The earring also follows the gesture of the woman. If we look closely at exhibit A, we can see how different it is from exhibit B. The earring in A has no brightness or attention to detail.
4. The female figure conceived by Hemen Mazumdar enshrines the meaning and the symbolism of eternal femininity. What emerges in Hemen's portrayal of women is a figure that is developed in both its earthly and sacred dimensions. He constructs his female figures in a manner that gives them an almost sculptural grandeur. In exhibit B, the viewer can almost feel the softness of the fabric, which envelops a body that looks as soft as butter. The contours of the limbs achieve the same results as tightly fitting drapery would, while the colours successfully shape the luminous complexion, revealing the sublime feminine beauty. We have a completely different approach in the exhibit A, where the sari looks extremely rigid and the use of chiaroscuro is totally wrong.
5. Hemen Mazumdar was gifted with the rare ability of constructing a clear, simple beauty that lifts the sensuality of the female figure to the highest levels. If we carefully look at exhibit A, we can see how the blouse drapes the back of the lady is far from the softness highlighted in

the exhibit B, where the bright white blouse drapes delicately around the waist and enhances the idea of sacred sensuality. Furthermore, the cleanness with which sari is tied on the waist is far superior in exhibit B.

To be clear about our disclaimer. We are not claiming that exhibit A is a forgery. We do not have the provenance information for it, nor have we conducted any technical analysis, or examined it physically. At best, we can say that in our judgement, it is inconclusive. Perhaps Hemen may have painted version A when he was having a bad day. But, I would only acquire version B of the painting. Beyond this, as this is an academic exercise, we leave the readers to draw their own conclusions, and even disagree with us. If they wish access to version B, we are happy to facilitate that. We learn through informed expert debates.

In this context, it is interesting to reflect on authentication boards that have been constituted for artists or set up by artists' foundations. In 1968, the Rembrandt Research Project was established to authenticate the great artist's works. The predictable happened. The number of "approved" Rembrandts steadily dropped from around 688 in Valentiner's 1921 catalogue raisonné to 250 in the 1986 Tumpel catalogue raisonné. Are we to believe that Rembrandt with his talent and longevity (1606-1669) could only produce around 300 works that are currently attributed to him? In contrast, Van Gogh (1853-1890) has more than 850 oil paintings attributed to him over a relatively brief career, mostly painted during the last two years of his life.

The result of "group think" in committees leads to genuine works being excluded as it is easier to say "no" than "yes". Members who reject more are viewed as being more rigorous in their approach. No one comes to the defence of the poor dead artist. Some years ago, I observed this with a three-person panel set up to authenticate Rabindranath Tagore's paintings. If a genuine painting in one style is rejected, then of course, the other paintings by the artist in the same style must also be questioned. Not surprisingly, the Rembrandt Research Project has been declared a failure.

Beyond disagreements between experts, there is the fear of litigation. Since the difference in valuation between an artwork that is declared genuine versus a fake can run into millions, even tens of millions of dollars, the threat of litigation has made authentication boards unviable. To avoid excessive litigation costs that arise from being sued, experts are increasingly keeping their negative opinion to themselves and declaring artworks as inconclusive rather than fakes. Several authentication boards, including those for Alexander Calder, Andy Warhol, Jason Pollock, Jean-Michel Basquiat, Keith Haring and Roy Lichtenstein have either stopped authenticating artworks or disbanded to avoid potential legal exposure.

Certain family members of Indian artists have made a business out of issuing authentication certificates. Many Indian academics also issue "certificates". Personally, I do not accept these as having any value because of the explicit conflict of interest and the implicit expert attribution being accorded to these family members. Descendants of Indian artists have been known to call auction houses and declare upcoming lots "fake" when they have not been incentivized. Consequently, international auction houses are increasingly unwilling to accept certificates for Indian art, preferring to make their own judgments based on provenance and expert eye.

Without formal training and a scholarly immersion into the artist lifetime of work, I am skeptical about an individual's judgment. As David Hockney observed, "people need to look intensely, but they can't. They need to be shown how to". Beyond the scholarly aspect, individuals differ dramatically in how good of an "eye" they possess. Finally, as noted earlier, despite all of this, we must accept the fallibility of the experts as humans. This sometimes leads to the belief that technical analysis is a panacea for "proving" authenticity.

Technical analysis

Technical analysis has conclusively identified many important forgeries. However, it cannot provide a definitive answer about the attribution of any particular artwork as being genuine. Furthermore, it is usually an expensive effort, so a thorough technical analysis is only viable for valuable works. It is easier to justify it for an old master like Titian (c. 1488/90-1576) valued in the millions versus a Kalighat painting that sells for £2,000. However, this area continues to evolve with more sophisticated and cost-effective tools becoming increasingly available.

Even before we had digital tools, x-rays, infrared spectroscopy and so on, less sophisticated technical methods were popular with authenticators. Oil paintings exhibit the telltale signs of age as it takes oil paint years to completely dry. Some authenticators have the ability to touch a painting to feel how soft versus hard the paint is, and thereby, assess whether it was painted recently. Using a dab of alcohol is an old trick, as oil paint that is not dry will dissolve.

Examining paintings under X-ray, UV light, and increasingly powerful microscopes allows for greater study of the surface, the pigments used, and what lies underneath a painting. One can investigate how the paint has been layered and whether the paint or the signature was added later. Pentimenti, the presence of earlier drawings, images, or strokes that have been altered or painted over, helps determine if the painting is the work of the original artist, the workshop, or a later copyist. Generally, copies will have few pentimenti compared to original works, especially for artists like Caravaggio, Rembrandt, and Titian, who preferred to compose directly on the canvas without preliminary drawings. Of course, this is not going to help us for an artist like Hemen Mazumdar, who copied himself over time. Later versions of the same composition would logically be expected to have few pentimenti compared to the initial one.

The process of aging leaves tempera and especially oil paintings with craquelure, a fine network of dense cracks. This crack formation due to the differential shrinkage across the painting surface is propagated by variations in humidity. If embedded with cracks, recent forged works have smoother texture and are more uniform than authentic older artworks where the irregular cracks are sharper and deeper. Induced cracks usually have signs of being filled in with pencil, charcoal, or India ink.

Earlier these cracks would be examined by sight, but now a topographical map of the painting can be created via Reflectance Transformation Imaging. Craquelure is like the fingerprint of an old painting. Paintings from different locations and times, produced in different styles, create unique craquelure patterns that are incredibly difficult to replicate in a fake. How cracks should have developed in oil paintings for Italian panels between 1300 and 1500 versus Flemish panels from 1400 to 1600 or Dutch canvases of the 1600s, are now well documented. However, such models do not exist for the more recent Indian modern art like Early Bengal Oils or Hemen Mazumdar. As their market value increases and more scholars of Indian art graduate, this will become inevitable. If forensic analysis of the paint on an artwork demonstrates that the paint had not been invented during the lifetime of the artist, or from when the painting is dated, then it is clearly a forgery. For example, Wofgang Beltracchi applied a titanium white in forging a 1914 work by Heinrich Campendonk (1889-1957), a paint that would not have existed then. Subsequently, it was uncovered that he had created hundreds of paintings, of masters such as Paul Gauguin and Édouard Manet, and even managed to have them placed in prestigious institutions like MoMA. Similarly, the paints used in the Knoedler Gallery fakes of Mark Rothko, Jackson Pollock, and so on, by a Chinese forger in New York were inconsistent with those used by the artists to whom the works were attributed.

Infrared spectroscopy and Raman spectroscopy are now fairly common. Without getting into technical details, Raman identified that each paint colour and pigment scatters light in a unique manner. Raman spectroscopy allows identification of the paints used in a particular artwork. One can then assess the overlap between these paints and those that were available during the time to which the painting is attributed, or favoured by the artist in their body of work. While having pigments that were unknown in the artist's lifetime verifies that the artwork is a forgery, the presence of historically appropriate pigments does not prove the opposite.

More recently, artificial intelligence (AI) and digital analysis have been deployed to help determine authenticity. By feeding all the known paintings of an artist into a database, algorithms developed for this purpose should be able to identify the complex unique pattern of an artist's brush strokes and style. However, this requires a large number of artworks from an artist to create the database, necessitating the cooperation of museums and collectors. Currently, such algorithms exist for a few artists like Van Gogh, Rubens, Monet, and Gauguin. It is a niche solution, which will become more important as AI becomes pervasive.
Non-Fungible Tokens (NFT) can help with recent and future artworks as they allow for the entire provenance history to be on a blockchain (provided the initial inputs are correct). Every movement of the artwork is documented, transparent, and unalterable by any individual. But we still need an infallible method of marking physical objects with a digital imprint so they cannot be replaced after being recorded on the blockchain.

Concluding Thoughts of a Bengal School Collector

I have been collecting art for over three decades, during which, I have probably acquired 500 artworks. Without exception, I have never observed the item being produced, rarely met the artist since my collection is primarily the work of those who are deceased, and frequently encountered works with gaps in provenance documentation. Therefore, after some due diligence, I have taken a leap of faith.

The best I can do now is to allow serious academics open access to the works and facilitate further research on their authenticity. Recall, we cannot prove beyond doubt that an artwork is authentic, only the opposite, that it is a forgery. In submitting my collection to academic scrutiny, one hopes that observers recognize that there is no intention to deceive or I would limit exposure of the artworks. And in this process, I recognize that some of the works may not be attributed to the artist that I have believed until now to be the master behind the artwork. However, unlike some modern art which is prized for its social status enhancing signature value, these artworks were acquired for their intrinsic merit, their magnificence, which will remain unchanged regardless of any attribution.

An intense conversation with Indian modern art history led me to understand the transformational role of the artists included in the Painting Freedom exhibition. The Bengal School artists were then yearning to break free of imposed Western conceptions of "fine art" as well as avoid becoming buried under five thousand years of inherited Indian art. These works embody the cry of an oppressed nation struggling to emerge as free and modern. As Paul Klee argued, a painting can be both immediately perceived and progressively understood.[14] These paintings pack layers of time- connecting the past, the then present, and coming future of Indian art. The backstory behind them and the dense invisible coating of history is what makes them exceptional in the annals of Indian modern art.

Yet, despite their historical significance, they did not, and still do not command the prices they should. Partially, it was the fear of "fakes" circulating within the Bengal School art market that enabled me to amass this collection. Otherwise, it would have been far beyond my means. From a financial perspective, to have been an in-depth collector of this unfashionable art can be considered either visionary or foolhardy. Regardless, for three decades, it has fueled my hunger for knowledge and the development of an eye. It demanded that I become a scholar and a devotee of this critical period of Indian modern art.

Orchestrating this collection, the works themselves as well as the process of acquiring art and educating myself, have brought tremendous joy. It has been an all-consuming passion, perhaps some may contend, madness. Even after all these years, the paintings continue to astonish me whenever I enter my London apartment. They are beloved by me and if further research deems some of them as "fakes", it would not lower my appreciation for them. Furthermore, in such a circumstance, no one except me needs to absorb any related financial losses. Fortunately, it is not going to change the quality of the wine that I open with dinner for the rest of my life. This art belongs to India and the world, I am just a temporary custodian preserving history. I will be gone someday, but the art will remain for others to enjoy, research, and judge.

Exhibit A: Finishing Touch

Exhibit B: Finishing Touch by Hemen Mazumdar

1 - Nicole Martinez, "Can you spot a fake? The trouble with authenticating art," Art Law Journal, 7 January 2021; Tips from an AXA art expert on art authentication, https://fineartmultiple.com/blog/axa-art-expert-authentication/

2 - Henri Neuendorf, "Why do contemporary artists use so many studio assistants?" www.artnet.com, 14 July 2016, https://news.artnet.com/art-world/art-demystified-the-use-of-assistants-549284

3 - Conversation with Debabrata Roy, eldest grandson of Jamini Roy, June 2021

4 - Bengal to Baker Street in 80 Paintings, Mukti Jain Champion, BBC Radio 4, first broadcast on 6 March 2014, https://www.bbc.co.uk/programmes/b03wq2sp

5 - Is this a Rembrandt? 26 May 2014, https://www.arthistorynews.com/articles/2809_Is_this_by_Rembrandt

6 - Conversation with Amitabh Banerjee, artist, born 1929 and also a graduate of Government College of Arts in Calcutta, who first visited Jamini Roy's home to buy an artwork.

7 - Brian Sewell, "Damien Hirst, Tate Modern", Exhibition review, Evening Standard, 5 April 2012, https://www.standard.co.uk/culture/exhibitions/damien-hirst-tate-modern-brian-sewell-s-review-7618751.html

8 - Daniel Grant, "Can artists really disown their early work?" Huffington Post, 25 May, 2011, https://www.huffpost.com/entry/can-artists-really-disown_b_678184

9 - Peter Landesman, "A 20th-Century Master Scam, New York Times, 18 July 1999, https://archive.nytimes.com/www.nytimes.com/library/magazine/home/19990718mag-art-forger.html

10 - Christopher Sharrock, Giovanni Morelli and Connoisseurship," 28 September 2019, https://medium.com/@plus4/giovanni-morelli-and-connoisseurship-395156ed3d90

11 - David D. Kirkpatrick and Elaine Sciolino, "A Clash of Wills Keeps a Leonardo Masterpiece Hidden," 11 April 2021, https://www.nytimes.com/2021/04/11/arts/design/salvator-mundi-louvre-leonardo.html

12 - https://coolcolors.lbl.gov/LBNL-Pigment-Database/database.html

13 - Barbara Wall, "Holding the Line Against Forgeries," The New York Times, 29 October 2009, https://www.nytimes.com/2009/10/29/business/global/29iht-nwsmart29.html

14 - Ariella Budick, Stanley Whitney, Studio Museum, Harlem, New York - review, Financial Times, 3 September 2015, https://www.ft.com/content/6bb6d7b8-5165-11e5-b029-b9d50a74fd14

Sunayani Devi (1875- 1962)

Shilpi Das

Belonging to a family of esteemed writers and painters of Tagore Household of Calcutta, Sunayani Devi was born to Saudamini Devi and Gunendranath Tagore. She was Rabindranath Tagore's niece and younger sister of legendary painters Abanindranath Tagore (1871-1951), a pioneer of the Bengal School of Art, and Gaganendranath Tagore (1867-1938), radical satirist and self-styled cubist. Interestingly, despite being a daughter of the artistically acclaimed Tagore Family, an abode of the Bengali Renaissance of the late nineteenth and twentieth century, Sunayani Devi was an autodidact in art. When her two elder brothers Abanindranath Tagore and Gaganendranth Tagore, were busy cultivating and renovating their own artistic skills, Sunayani Devi excelled in her painting skill without any institutional training in academic realism; she tutored herself by watching her two elder brothers practising art, experimenting with various art forms.

Sunayani mentioned that as a child, she was fascinated by the devotional pictures that hung in her aunt's room, the Ravi Varma prints making the strongest impression on her. Spying on her two older brothers' experiments in Japanese wash techniques, she secretly longed to pick up the brush and paint. However, in her thirties, it was not until after being motivated by her husband, Rajanimohan Chattopadhyay (grandson of Raja Rammohan Roy), that she had engrossed herself thoroughly in artistic activities. She continued pursuing her passion on a larger scale, the predominant themes of her paintings being the subjects and the objects of everyday life that had surrounded her. During her fifteen active years (between the age of 30 to 45), she maintained a strict painting regimen, working every day from eight in the morning until midday and then from three until four-thirty.

The subject matter of Sunayani's art belonged to a private inner world. 'Most of my paintings,' she once confessed to her grandson, Kishore Chatterjee, 'I have seen in dreams – after seeing them, I have put them down.'[1] Her paintings which are individualised as naive, were perhaps born due to the anti-colonial resistance that she had imbibed for being nurtured in an environment imbued in Swadeshi ideals, where her elder brother Abanindranath Tagore advocated for the revival of Indian Art. Like her contemporary male peers, we may boldly claim that Sunayani was competent enough to form a school of painting of her own.

The paintings displayed in the current exhibition exemplify how Sunayani Devi had borrowed the stereotypes of Indian women from the inner quarters and depicted them with vibrant colours in her own individualistic style. That Sunayani Devi had a loving husband who had played an active and progressive role in the proliferation of her artistic growth is oft-discussed in the context of

Sunayani Devi's emergence as one of the first women artists of early-twentieth-century India. Her paintings, too, communicate the same. The repetition of the artist's Shiva-Parvati theme in her paintings conveys how deep and strong her marital bond was. In this exhibition, too, two of her paintings portray Shiva and Parvati in one single frame.

In 1922, Sunayani's paintings were exhibited in the prestigious Fourteenth Annual Exhibition of the Indian Society of Oriental Art in Calcutta, in which the Bauhaus artists took part. In 1925, The Statesman wrote approvingly that she showed vigour and originality although she was a woman. The Englishman commented on the bold originality of her paintings, which resembled ancient Jain paintings in their hieratic quality. In 1927, she was included in the Women's International Art Club exhibition in London. At the Twenty-Sixth Annual Exhibition (1934-1935) of the Indian Society of Oriental Art, Calcutta, seven paintings by Sunayani Devi - *Krishna and Jasoda, The King and the Queen, Innocence, The Poet, The Eternal Cow Boy, Krishna and Radha* were exhibited. Also, among several other women artists, Sunayani's painting *Sree Radha* was exhibited at the *Exhibition of Indian Drawings, Paintings and Drypoints* at Suri Townhall 1945. Sunayani was the only woman artist to show two of her paintings in the *Indian Exhibition* held in Singapore, 1948. During the 1940s, her family suffered a series of misfortunes that had caused her deep despair. The outcome being her departure from the world of art. With her husband's death in 1934, Sunayani Devi lost all her vigour to paint.

Dr Stella Kramrisch, an authority of Indian art and Hinduism and the first professor of Indian Art at the University of Calcutta (1923), became Sunayani's powerful champion, providing the first serious study of the artist. She introduced Sunayani Devi to the larger world as the first Indian modern woman artist of India. To Kramrisch, her limited skill and narrow horizon were a strength rather than weakness, a form of naïve grandeur. Ravi Varma's prints thrilled her, and later she saw Rajput miniatures and Abanindranath's watercolours. However, in line with the growing cult of folk art, Kramrisch identified only two main inspirations: village clay dolls that often adorned urban homes and Kalighat pats.[2]

The Austrian painter Nora Pursar Wuttenbrach, who contributed the catalogue essay on her, was charmed by the lotus-eyed women and enchanting colours. She was impressed by the monumental fresco-like quality of these small paintings. She had met Sunayani during her visit to Calcutta to produce murals for a local Art Deco movie theatre.[3]

According to renowned art historian Partha Mitter, 'rather than describing her as a folk painter, we should view her as a genuine naïve painter who used folk motifs with immense charm and feeling.'[4] In the words of art critic Gayatri Sinha, "A precursor of folk art in the fine art tradition, she anticipated the more full-blown realisation of Jamini Roy (1887-1972)."[5] Here is an interesting incident of how deeply Jamini Roy was grateful to her. Once Sunayani had attended an inaugural ceremony of an art education centre named "Kalabharati" as an audience where Jamini Roy was the chief guest, seated on the dais. Jamini Roy, chancing upon Sunayani Devi among the audience, came down to her immediately, held her by his hands and ushered her respectfully to his seat. Jamini had spontaneously enquired in a tone implying disapproval, "Despite her presence here, why have I been conferred this position?". Such profound was his level of reverence towards Sunayani Devi![6]

Despite the presence of umpteen women artists in Indian art history and the Bengal School, they remain vastly underrepresented. Although women across India and several corners of the world received formal art training at Kala Bhavan, Santiniketan, the art domain being an exclusively male-dominated space, the male artists and the male art students were essentially the prime movers. Sunayani Devi, being part of the more enlightened and elite Tagore and Roy households, has received more and more attention since her era from the art world. Besides Sunayani Devi, several other women artists had overcome familial and societal obstacles. Also, like her, they had shared close attachment with the Jorasanko Tagores- Pratima Tagore, Chitranibha Chowdhury, Rani Chanda, Hasirashi Devi, Atasi Barua, to name a few of them. However, even though we reached the twenty-first century, the only woman artist of early-twentieth-century Bengal people are aware of and is exhibited all around is Sunayani Devi. Although she has left an inedible mark on the emergence of Indian modern art, she is represented scantily in the museum collections (Indian Museum and Victoria Memorial in Kolkata and the National Gallery of Modern Art in Delhi and Bangalore).

1 - Chatterjee, Kishore, "Sunayani Devi", in Ashok Bhattacharya (ed.), *Charukala*, Rajya Charukala Parshad, 2000: 65-68.

2 - https://criticalcollective.in/ArtistInner2.aspx?Aid=546&Eid=575

3 - Ibid.

4 - Mitter Partha, *The Triumph of Modernism: India's artists and the avant-garde, 1922–1947*, Oxford University Press, 2007: 44.

5 - Sinha Gayatri, "Women artists in India: practice and patronage" in D. Cherry, J. Helland (eds.), *Local/Global: Women Artists in the Nineteenth Century*, Taylor & Francis, 2006.

6 - Deb, Chitra *Thakurbarir Andarmahal*, Ananda Publishers Private Limited, ed. 8th, 2016: 123.

Information related to Sunayani Devi's exhibited works have been procured from Mukul Dey Archives

The Original Copy

Sona Datta

The subject of copying in art is neither new nor simple.[1] It remains pervasive in contemporary culture yet subject to legal restrictions and societal taboos that continually imply it is morally or ethically subversive. In today's capitalist economies, platonic mimesis is fully entangled with modern memes and Western art is forever debating the charged space between the *original* and the *copy*, especially with reference to fine art and its collectors, its forgeries and the monetary value of the all-powerful and 'original', work of art.

There was a time when *to publish* signified making an original text available for scholars to copy, a process that would enable students to engage fully with the material. So a book that was *not* copied was one that would probably be lost to humanity. The world of cultural production is thus embedded with multitudes of copies that are amount to more than mere imitations. When Andy Warhol declared his role in the drama of western modernism, his creative appropriations elevated artistic copy to a pivotal role in the contemporary zeitgeist. The centrality of copying in the human creative project remains present and undeniable. Historically, there have been many arguments about what constitutes great art. In India, as in Europe since the Renaissance, artists were trained by copying the work of others. However, it was of course the Renaissance that also demanded the artist achieve recognition as an innovator, and not merely as an imitator.

Western art's uniqueness has thus been predicated on the notion that it cannot be reproduced. In both traditional and contemporary art, originality conferred upon the object an aura of the sacred simultaneously transforming the museum into a sanctum. In pre-capitalist society works of art were part of a system of collective labour, namely the *guild* or *karkhana* with artisans or *karigars*. This form of cultural production involved a particular kind of patronage, one in which value was calculated on the basis of materials used rather than on skill alone.[2] The modern post-industrial art market disrupted the guild system and the artist now faced the market armed only with his skill which was hall-marked by his signature.[3]

The core ambition of the British art curriculum in colonial India was 'to teach *them* (the Indians) one thing, which through all the preceding ages they have never learnt, namely drawing objects correctly, whether figures, landscape or architecture'.[4] For Richard Temple and others in the landscape of nineteenth century colonial India, drawing meant the exact copying of old masters, and the imitation of reality with precision and exactitude. While the Indian artist may have been described as proficient in deploying ornament and design, he was also perceived as lacking the requisite 'scientific' skills to produce mimetic copies of nature.[5] But the point missed here was that Indian art had never really concerned itself with reality. Why would it, when one had reality in multitudes all around one? Fundamentally, Indian art had always been about the *landscape of the imagination*.

Slavish copying in the colonial art schools was perhaps best exemplified in John Griffiths' twelve-year project at Ajanta while he was principal of the JJ School of Art in Bombay. For more than a decade, Griffiths engaged his students to produce meticulous copies of the great murals found within the caves at Ajanta.[6] However, some of his students refused to participate believing the task would stifle their creativity. Indeed, Pestonji Bomnaji, who would become one of India's most famed oil painters, would deny in later life that he had ever worked at Ajanta.[7]

The early twentieth century in India, and especially in Bengal, saw the revivalism of the Bengal School centred around Abanindranath Tagore and the 'culture-castle' of the Tagores at Jorasankho in North Calcutta pitted against a growing popularity of academic realism best exemplified by artists such as Jamini Gangooly and Hemendranath Mazumdar.
Following the upheaval around Curzon's first Partition of Bengal in 1905, Percy Brown's replacement of Havell as principal of the Government College of Arts in Kolkata enabled the reintroduction of academic naturalism into the school's curriculum. Mazumdar, Jamini Roy and Atul Bose went on to establish the *Indian Academy*, a convivial forum that debated the big questions of the day, namely whether 'the pursuit of naturalism in art was tantamount to a betrayal of national ideals and whether the historicism of the Bengal school was the sole path to India's artistic revival'.[8]

Theorist Homi Bhabha's focus on the space between 'mockery and mimicry' and its role in revealing 'colonial ambivalence' has been deeply influential in discussions around cultural representation, becoming a bedrock in discussion of post-colonial criticism.[9]

While Jamini Roy would eventually reject both academic realism and the artistic objectives of the Bengal School, Mazumdar would remain fiercely and vocally opposed to orientalism until his dying day asserting instead the universal nature of academic art. Thus, by 1921, Mazumdar's prodigious output had created an entirely new genre of figure painting in India, one that delighted in the sensuous, almost sexualised, qualities of the female flesh of the unattainable upper class elite Bengali woman. Mazumdar's Bengali woman clad in a 'wet sari' became his signature style, and fed the repressed and hungry desires of the Bengali middle classes who stood as much by a sense of received English prudery as by a revulsion that rendered them incapable of appreciating India's own rich traditions of erotic temple art.

Jamini Roy, on the other hand, successfully drew on multiple sources from his own childhood and cultural oeuvre, transforming the language of Bengali folk art into the modernist project of picture making and deploying his works across the mantlepieces of metropolitan Kolkata.

While the Western classical nude would remain alien to the Indian eye, a work such as Mazumdar's *Dilli ka Laddu* or the 'Obscure Object of Desire' depicted a Bengali lady so familiar she could belong in everyone's family: Mazumdar thus placed sexual frisson almost within reach and became one of the few Indian artists of the early twentieth century to reap both financial and critical reward for his painting.[10] His depictions of women salute the continuity of an unbroken tradition that actually stretches back two millenia to the fecund Indian tree spirit or *Yakshi*, exemplified by the famous sandstone figure from the 1st century in the British Museum's collection.[11]

'Jamini Roy signifies not just the advent of modern art in India, but the advent of the modern Indian artist. There is a special relationship between the identities of 'modern' and 'Indian' which is uniquely tied to the historical moment. Jamini Roy's painting was modern because he created a new and distinct style and it was Indian because of its 'technique and conception'.[12]

And despite their variant practices, both Jamini Roy and Hemen Mazumdar would repeat many of their most popular works in different sizes and media. Indian art and philosophy has always had a clear sphere of application and so the pragmatist in each of them undoubtedly led them to surmise that this kind of production was also an opportune market-based response. Mazumdar was repeatedly requested by the maharajas of India's princely states to deliver them their own version of his most famous works alongside portraits of family members (the latter by definition were unique). Similarly, for Jamini Roy's buyers, such a request was clearly also a strategy to infiltrate the middle class home.

Vishaka Desai notes that in the 'modernist and historiographical bias in favour of 'original' creations by 'individual' artists...not much attention has been paid to understanding the nature of the more fundamental aspect of Indian painting: namely, the continuity of tradition and the process of using earlier works for the creation of new images".[13] Following the development of the Mughal atelier in the sixteenth century, the names of a few key artists came to the fore and so the idea of a 'unique' work by an individual took root in a modest way within the Indian tradition. However, beyond discussions of stylistic connections and continuities, there has been no contextual discourse on the subject of copies that considers such important questions as the cultural and non-stylistic connections between the model and its copies, or in the function of copies in creating art works and their role as a definitive link to the past.[14]

In this sense, copying could elevate a new work by giving it a secure link to the past. Indeed, Indian art is expanded through an ideological mechanism that acts by inclusion, producing different results each time. The singular characteristic of such a process is that the ancient returns in the modern reintroducing it in a different context, thus creating a 'connective tissue that nourishes Indian art as a whole'.[15]

Desai describes how much of pre-modern Indian painting was concerned with copying, following established models rather than a wholehearted and agonistic turn away from tradition. Thus, within the context of the Indian tradition, artists never set out to make exact replicas; but were simply working within a traditional framework of an established model, and making it current in a variety of ways. Thus in the Indian painting tradition, the most common form of the copying process involved uninterrupted referents to the past through a work's structure and composition, whereas details of clothing, furnishing and decoration served to bring the past up to the present within the same work. The intention, then, was not simply to reproduce the original but to create a continuity between the past and the present.[16]

Historically, Indian visual and musical arts shared a core structure that the individual practitioner then improvised upon, famously seen in musical ragas and their painted equivalents. Therein lay the scope and terrain for individuality. In this sense, creativity is viewed as a kind of improvisation rather than self-conscious expression. The individual calling for the artist-genius was thus not one that was visited upon artists in India before the twentieth century.

The traditional artist's practice was thus the product of a habitual practice. Apprentices patiently copy the gestures of the master until the techniques of their craft had been internalised.[17] This alone allowed them to secure deep knowledge about how the material behaved in the hands of the craftsman enabling them to develop a set of templates that could be adapted to different creative cues, thus creating work of aesthetic value despite limited conceptual knowledge.[18]

Colonisation had alienated Indians from traditional visual culture and so the reclamation of the folk, the craft and the subaltern became an integral part of the post-colonial project. At Santiniketan, Rabindranath Tagore introduced an arts curriculum driven by medieval and folk art and principles of utility. Tagore's was a *contextual modernism*, that is not a modernism borne of a continuity of style but one borne through a community of ideas.

In the modern period, Jamini Roy managed to harness two paradoxical standpoints: namely, the assimilation of a folk idiom from a continuous tradition with the idea of himself as the organisational source and master of the work – a unique individual with a distinctly personal style. Thus, for Roy, the Bengali vernacular was deeply embroiled in the nationalist fight for *swaraj*.[19]

As Partha Mitter so beautifully sums up, '*what the cognoscenti failed to grasp is Roy's radical critique of colonialism through his art. Through his own artistic objectives, this supreme individualist voluntarily returned to the anonymity of tradition*'.[20]

1 - Boon. M, In Praise of Copying, Cambridge, 2010.

2 - 1. M. Baxandell, *Painting and Experience in Fifteenth Century Italy*, Oxford, 1972: 5-8.

3 - R. Chatterjee, 'The Original Jamini Roy': A Study in the Consumerism of Art, *Social Scientist*, Vol. 15, No. 1 (Jan., 1987: 3-18.

4 - Richard Temple, *Oriental Experience* (1883), p.485 cited in Mathur, India By Design, p. 94

5 - Saloni Mathur, *India by Design*, 2007: 93-4

6 - John Griffiths, Report on the Work of Copying the Paintings of the Ajanta Caves (London 1872-85).

7 - Mitter, Art and Nationalism in Colonial India, p.54

8 - Mitter, *The Triumph of Modernism*, p.129

9 - Homi Bhabha, *The Location of Culture*, New York, 1994.

10 - By 1921, he had won the prestigious gold medal for his painting *Reminiscence* at a Mumbai exhibition as well as the first prize at the Society of Fine Arts in Kolkata.

11 - Yakshi, 1st century sandstone, British Museum 1842,1210.1

12 - S. Datta, Urban Patua, 2010: 91

13 - V.N. Desai, 'Reflections of the Past in the Present: Copying Processes in Indian Painting" in Asher & Metcalf, eds. *Perceptions of South Asia's Visual Past*, p.135.

14 - For literature on the concept of copies, particularly with regard to postmodern scholarship in western art history, see Richard Shiff, "Representation, Copying and the Technique of Originality" in New Literary History. 15 (2 (Winter 1984), pp.331-363; and Rosalind Kraus (ed.), *Retaining the Originals Multiple Originals, Copes and Reproductions* (Washington 1989).

15 - P. Maiullari, "Jamini Roy and the Mimetic Origin of Indian Art" in C. Corni (ed.), *Jamini Roy, From Tradition to Modernity – the Kumar Collection*, Lugano 2015:52

16 - Desai, op.cit: 144.

17 - Farr, James R. 2008. *The Work of France: Labour and Culture in Early Modern Times, 1350-1800*. London: Rowman and Littlefield.

18 - Siva Kumar, R. 2006. "K.G. Subramanyan's Saras." In Sahmat Artists Alert, *Iconography Now. Rewriting Art History*. 86-90. Delhi: Sahmat.

19 - Datta, *Urban Patua*, 2010: 91.

20 - Mitter, *The Triumph of Modernism*, 2007: 120.

Early Bengal
OILS
1850s - 1910s

Europeans artists began arriving in India from the 16th century onwards. They brought a style (western academic with an emphasis on perspective and light) and a medium (oil on canvas) that was alien to India. These European artists were patronized by the colonial aristocracy and local rulers in India.

Visiting European artists depicted Indian subjects using the terms of European academic realism. To meet growing demand for their new style of painting, they trained Indian miniature painters as "assistants". During the 19th Century, Bengal's aristocrats invited such Indian artists to instead paint popular Indian mythological and religious subjects. This unique East-West 'fusion' is referred to as Early Bengal Oils. While these painters reached into the Western technique of oil, their works remained Indian in spirit.

Early Bengal Oils are usually dated between the mid 1850s until the beginning of the 20th century. Wealthy patrons moved from these Early Bengal Oils to supporting the more modern artists of the Orientalist Bengal School emerging from Calcutta's Government College of Art.

Goddess Jagaddhatri (literally meaning bearer of the world) is one of the incarnations of Goddess Durga and is considered to represent qualities of positivity and virtuousness. The depiction of Jagaddhatri and her vehicle, the lion, crushing the elephant is symbolic of her destroying the ego of all the male Gods and Devas, who doubted the powers of a woman. In the painting, men belonging to varying social classes, including priests, a sage and a man dressed like a typical courtier of the Murshidabad region of then Bengal are seen paying their respects, symbolizing the goddess's superiority.

Untitled, (Jagaddhatri)
Oil on canvas, 76 x 61 cm

Krishna and Balaram were not blood brothers, but they were raised by the same parents. They grew up as great friends and herded cows together. In the painting, they are seen enjoying a moment of peace where Krishna is playing his flute and Balarama is accompanying him on an instrument made from an animal horn.

Untitled, (Krishna and Balarama)
Oil on canvas, 76 x 59 cm

Annapurna is the Hindu goddess of food and nourishment. During an argument with his wife Parvati, Lord Shiva remarked how material things, including food, were just an illusion. To prove her point, Parvati disappeared with all material things. As earthlings suffered without food, Shiva realised his mistake and went begging to Parvati, who, in the form of Annapurna, was distributing food.

Untitled, (Annapurna giving alms)
Oil on canvas, 45 x 35 cm

For Early Bengal Oils and Kalighat School paintings, we cannot identify the artists behind the works or their dates accurately. These artists painted timeless Indian stories. The same image was executed repeatedly, within and across generations. Consistent with Indian artistic traditions, they did not claim personal ownership of the works or locate them at a particular time having inherited the idea, even if the details evolved ever so slowly.

Untitled, (Krishna & Radha)
Oil on canvas, 76 x 59 cm

This painting depicts the coronation Lord Rama, hero of the Indian epic, The Ramayana. It signifies the commencement of his taking up the responsibilities of the world by becoming consecrated as a king. 'Ram-Rajya' has now become an idiom which means a kingdom/state which is perfectly governed.

Untitled, (Coronation of Rama)
Oil on canvas, 75 x 57 cm

The painting represents the holy trinity of Hindu mythology: Brahma (The Creator), Vishnu (The Preserver), and Shiva (The Destroyer), aligned with the King of the Serpents, Seshnaga. Seshnaga, whose name means "that which remains" is floating in an Ocean of Bliss, shaped as the seraphic 'Om'. Goddess Lakshmi, Vishnu's wife is sitting at his feet, since she has vowed to serve Vishnu her entire life.

Untitled, (Vishnu as Seshashayee with Seshnag in form of Om)
Oil on canvas, 72 x 47 cm

Untitled, (Krishnalila)
Oil on canvas, 61 x 90.5 cm

Several women known as 'Gopis' offered unconditional devotion to Krishna. The 'Krishna Charit' describes the devotion of sixteen thousand Gopinis, with nine primary ones. They are generally divided into three groups: friends of similar age to Krishna; maidservants; and messengers. The painting has the divine couple Krishna and Radha surrounded by the inner circle of Gopis.

Untitled, (Kali)
Mixed media on paper, 41 x 28 cm

The Hindu goddess Kali represents time and death ('Kal' meaning time). In one legend, after defeating a powerful demon army, Kali bloodlust becomes out of control. To reinstate universal order her husband, Lord Shiva, laid down on her path. In her wrath, Kali unknowingly stepped on him. Realising her mistake, she immediately calmed down. Her outstretched tongue symbolises her shame and embarrassment at stepping on her husband. In the 1970s, as an anti-authoritarian act of rebellion, the Rolling Stones used Kali's protruding tongue as their logo.

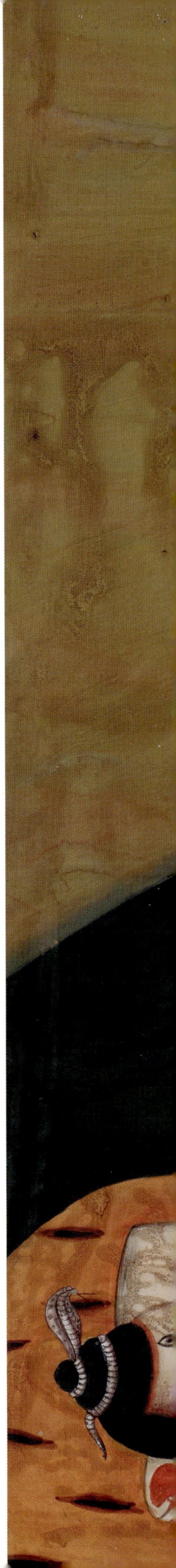

ষোড়শী

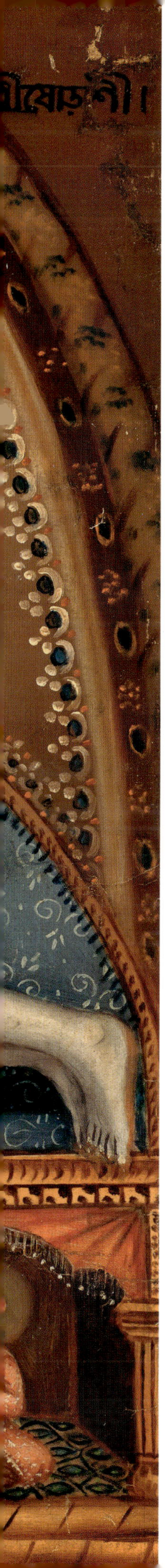

Untitled
Oil on canvas, 103 x 82 cm

Tripura Sundari, also known as Shodasi, is another form of Kali. She is depicted seated on a throne, whose legs comprise of Brahma, Vishnu, Shiva, and Rudra. In Shaktism, the goddess oriented sect of Hinduism, this represents supreme consciousness, ruling above the other gods. She lies on top of a supine Shiva, seated on a lotus that is growing out of Shiva's navel.

Untitled (Shiva and Kamdev))
Oil on canvas, 75 x 61 cm

Bengal Pats

Patuas, the folk painters from Bengal, have been painting for generations, possibly since as early as the 13th century. Patuas worked by traveling from village to village with paintings of religious stories done on scrolls. The most popular subjects were the two Indian epics, Ramayana and Mahabharata, as well as the lives of popular Islamic saints.

In each village, they would sing songs narrating the stories while unfurling their work. This created a dynamic oral tradition enhanced by visual art. Their objective was not to sell their artwork. Instead they made their living from donations for their performances, often making appearances at local fairs.

Untitled
Watercolour on paper mounted on cloth, 204 x 28.5 cm

Untitled
Watercolour on paper mounted on cloth, 230 x 19 cm

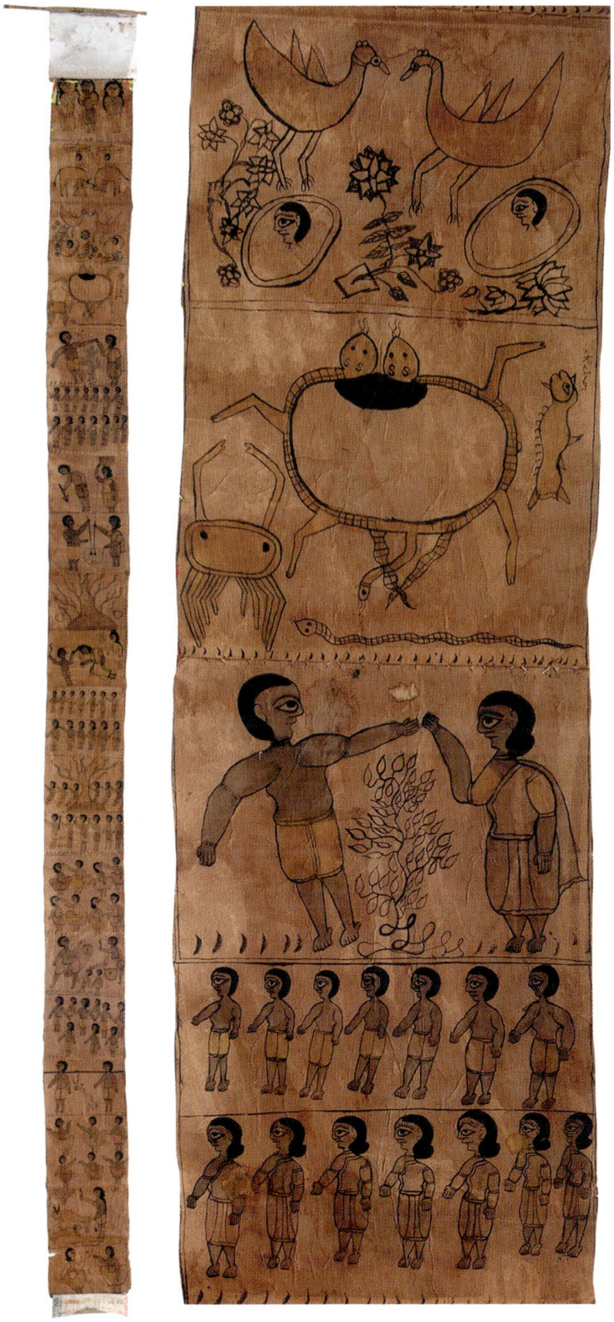

Untitled
Ink on paper mounted on cloth, 285 x 19.5 cm

Untitled
Watercolour on canvas, 335 x 31 cm

The scroll depicts various scenes from the life of the Hindu god, Krishna. Krishna's parents were jailed by his evil maternal uncle Kansa, who wanted to kill every offspring of theirs, leading to the prophecy that the eighth child would be the cause of Kansa's death. Krishna grew up in Gokul with his foster parents and is affectionately imagined as a very naughty child. For example, he is presented as playing with his brother, Balaram, stealing the clothes of unsuspecting women when bathing in a stream or stealing his favourite "makhan" (home-made butter).

Kalighat School
1850s - 1930s

By the nineteenth century, the Kalighat temple on the banks of the River Hooghly in Calcutta had become an increasingly popular destination for Bengali pilgrims and artists. Kalighat painters mostly depicted religious subjects, but also often held up a humorous, even unforgiving, mirror to contemporary society.

Kalighat paintings were quickly produced, plentiful and affordable. They are celebrated for their powerful rhythmic strokes and paring down of detail, making them bold visual statements. Kalighat painting created a glorious anti-naturalist but realist original indigenous style, which is now considered by art historians to be the first Indian modern art.

The Kalighat School operating from the vicinity of the Kalighat temple thrived for period of 100 years from 1830s. The practice disappeared from Calcutta in the face of mass produced cheap commercial posters. While the artists returned to their villages, their descendants in the districts of Medinipur and Birbhum are still producing contemporary Kalighat paintings.

The 'Elokeshi Murder' was one of the biggest urban scandals in nineteenth century Bengal. Elokeshi, a sixteen year old housewife, lived in her maternal house far from her husband, Nobin Chandra, when she had an illicit affair with the Mahant (head-priest) of Tarakeshwar temple. This ultimately resulted in her being decapitated by her husband. The scandal garnered huge public attention. Nobin was released after two years of imprisonment, because of public sympathy towards a morally right husband punishing an unchaste wife. The Mahant continued to serve at the temple until his death.

Untitled, (Elokeshi seeks forgiveness)
Watercolour on paper, 39.5 x 31.5 cm

Untitled
Watercolour on paper, 24.5 x 18.5 cm

Untitled, (The Mahant fans Elokeshi)
Watercolour on paper, 32 x 23.5 cm

Untitled, (Tabla Player)
Watercolour on paper, 24.5 x 18.5 cm

Untitled, (Babu & Bibi)
Watercolour on paper, 37 x 24 cm

Untitled
Watercolour on paper, 45.5 x 29.5 cm

This painting stems from the metropolitan bazaar. Depicted as a middle-aged family man, the Hindu god, Shiva is on an outing. Using his damaru (drum) as a child's rattle, he attempts to entertain the infant Ganesha, while Parvati pacifies the child by clapping her hands. The down to earth and playful conception of a cultic image is characteristic of the genre.

Untitled, (Shiva, Parvati & Ganesh)
Watercolour on paper, 33 x 21.5 cm

Untitled, (Shiva & Ganesh)
Watercolour on paper, 35.5 x 25 cm

A characteristic example of the Kalighat milieu, this painting of Shiva's marriage is cast in the mould of the everyday middle-class wedding in Calcutta.

Untitled, (Shiva's Marriage)
Watercolour on paper, 37 x 26 cm

Untitled, (Cat and lobster)
Watercolour on paper, 46.5 x 27 cm

Untitled, (Shiva & Parvati on Nandi)
Watercolour on paper, 40 x 30 cm

Untitled, (Shiva Mahadeva)
Watercolour on paper, 34.5 x 26 cm

A popular legend has Shiva using various types of intoxication to escape the bubble of worldly illusions or 'maya'. Bhang, a traditional Indian beverage infused with cannabis is often associated with Shiva and his devotees. It is said to help Shiva focus inward, allowing him to harness his divine powers. This is believed to inculcate self-control and self-discipline.

Legend has it that through his penance, the buffalo demon, Mahishasura requested Brahma for immortality. But Brahma argued that everyone must die. Viewing women as weak, Mahishasura, asked that only a woman should be able to slay him. Thus, seeing himself as invincible, he unleashed a tirade against the heavens. To defeat Mahishasura, the mighty goddess Durga (the 'Unvanquishable') was created through a union of all the Gods' collective powers. Following a five-day battle, Durga emerged victorious. This fearless form of Durga as the protective mother is revered in Bengal.

Untitled, (Durga)
Watercolour on paper, 47 x 35.5 cm

Untitled, (Woman)
Black paint on paper, 40 x 24 cm

Untitled, (Doting Husband)
Black paint on paper, 34 x 26.5 cm

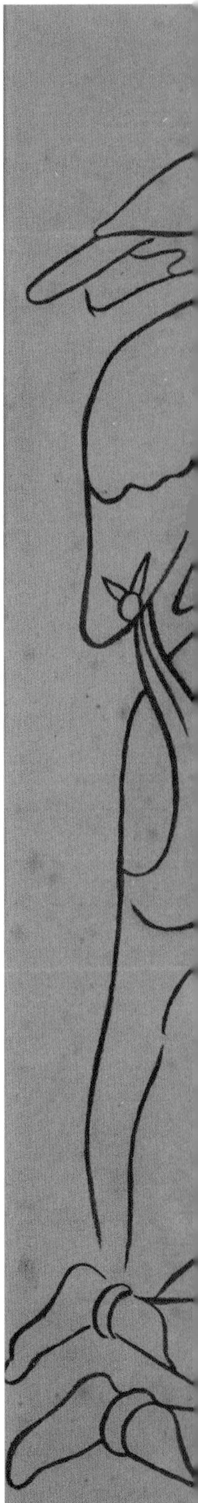

Untitled, (Babu & Bibi)
Black paint on paper, 25 x 18 cm

Untitled, (Shiva & Parvati)
Black paint on paper, 23 x 17.5 cm

Untitled, (Shiva)
Watercolour on paper, 50 x 33 cm

Western Academic

Academic art, introduced by the British Raj, was challenged by the nationalist art movement, the Orientalist Bengal School, led by Abanindranath Tagore and his disciples who dominated the art scene in the first decades of the twentieth century. Around 1915, academic artists had been in retreat all over India because of the Bengal School.

Atul Bose, Hemendranath Mazumdar, and Jamini Roy met as students at Calcutta's government art college and became close friends. The group decided to set up an academic artists' circle to challenge the onslaught of the Bengal School against academic artists. In 1920, the group brought out an influential illustrated journal, *Indian Academy of Art*, to win over the Bengali public. They also organised exhibitions to showcase academic artists from all around India, but the ultimate intention of the *Indian Academy of Art* was to publicise the works of Bose, Mazumdar and Jamini Roy. However, Jamini Roy, remained with them only for a while before eventually moving away from academic naturalism.

Atul Bose
1898-1977

Interested in the human form, Atul Bose chose to do portraiture early on. He got acquainted with European painting while studying at the Royal Art School, London. At a time when artists were following the Bengal 'School' style, Bose followed the realist mode. He laid emphasis on colour, line and tone whose harmonious blend made his canvases lifelike. In addition to bucolic landscapes, he often painted the harsh life of the common man, including a series on the Bengal Famine. In 1970, he was awarded a D.Litt by Rabindra Bharati University.

Untitled, (Nude)
Oil on canvas, 100 x 51 cm

Untitled, (Self Portrait)
Oil on canvas, 117 x 56 cm

Bamapada Banerjee
1851-1932

Bamapada Banerjee received his initial training in painting at the Calcutta Art School but, disillusioned with its pedagogy, he left and took private lessons with Pramathalal Mitra. Subsequently, he worked as an apprentice to the German painter Karl Becker who was then living in Calcutta. He received a prize in an exhibition organized by the Society for the Promotion of Industrial Art in 1879. From 1880 to 1884 he did commissions in Allahabad and Lahore. Bamapada Banerjee's popularity rests on his paintings illustrating Hindu mythology. He was deeply influenced by the genres of European history painting. Though a junior contemporary of Ravi Varma, the most influential artist of the time, Bamapada evolved an individual style and dominated the popular taste for decades through reproductions of his works, most of which were printed in Germany.

Untitled, Portrait, 1911
Oil on canvas, 60 x 50 cm

Mukul Dey
1895-1989

Introduced to printmaking by W. W. Pearson, Mukul Dey was one of the first artists to explore printmaking beyond its role as a tool of the colonial enterprise. Time spent at art schools in England deepened his interest in printmaking, and upon his return to India as the principal of Government School of Art, Calcutta, he actively promoted the medium. In 1916, he became the first Indian artist to be elected a member of the Chicago Society of Etchers and published several volumes of his etchings and illustrations in subsequent decades. From 1956 to '58, he served as curator of the National Gallery of Modern Art, New Delhi, and in 1987, he became a fellow of the Lalit Kala Akademi, New Delhi.

Rabindranath Tagore met Einstein several times, and famously, debated various subjects. The New York Times reported on one of their conversations in 1930 as "Einstein and Tagore plumb the truth". Tagore, as Mukul Dey's mentor, most probably introduced him to Einstein.

Untitled, (Einstien), 1926
Drypoint, 19 x 13.5 cm

Bengal School Orientalists

By 1900, Abanindranath Tagore (1871-1951) felt it was time to find an alternative well from which to source India's modernity. Nephew of the poet Rabindranath Tagore, Abanindranath led India's first nationalist art movement. The resulting Bengal School of Art was born at the Government College of Art in Calcutta.

Rejecting Western aesthetics, the Bengal School orientalists sought to be part of a pan-Asian movement fusing indigenous Hindu and Mughal painting styles with Japanese wash techniques. The ancient Buddhist site of Ajanta in Western India had been rediscovered in the nineteenth century. With its breath-taking murals, Ajanta became a national icon as India now realised it had its own 'glorious classical past'. Abinindranath's most promising student, Nandalal Bose (1882-1966), was sent to copy the Ajanta murals.

Abanindranath Tagore
1871-1951

Born in Jorasanko Thakur Bari, the ancestral home of the illustrious Tagore family, Abanindranath Tagore was the son of artist Gunendranath Tagore and nephew of the Nobel laureate Rabindranath Tagore. He studied at the Government School of Art, Calcutta, learnt painting under Olinto Ghilardi and Charles Palmer, and Japanese brushwork under Yokoyama Taikan. However, it was E. B. Havell, the principal of the Calcutta School of Art, who turned him towards the study of Mughal and Rajput painting, making Tagore an active proponent of nationalist revivalism in Indian art and founder of the Bengal 'School'. A highly influential teacher, Tagore taught a generation that reimagined the definition of modern art within the Indian context. He passed away on December 5, 1951.

Untitled, (Queen)
Watercolour on paper, 22.5 x 19.5 cm

Untitled, 1910
Watercolour on paper, 12 x 17 cm

Abanindranath Tagore was recruited to illustrate the first and best known English translation of The Rubaiyat of Omar Khayyam by Edward Fitzgerald. This painting exemplifies Tagore drawing from the Mughal miniature tradition.

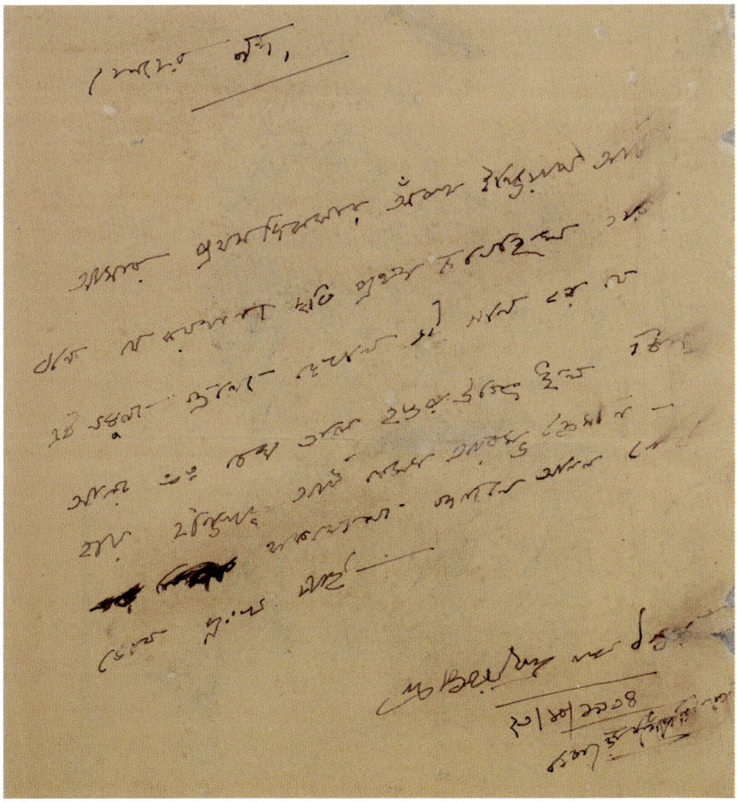

Untitled, (Rabindranath Tagore), 23/10/34
Pen and ink on paper, 21.5 x 13.5 cm

Dear Nanda *(to Nandalal Bose)*
When I come across these samples of those few paintings of my earlier phase that got widely popularized as Indian art for the very first time, I feel that they ought to have been finer. But alas! The way Indian art had been in its inception – let's put this aside, perhaps you have heard about the sad demise of Anil, this is extremely anguishing as I think about –

Signed: Sri Abanindranath Tagore

Untitled, (Bird)
Watercolour on paper, 18.5 x 12 cm

Asit Kumar Haldar
1890-1964

Born in Jorasanko, Calcutta, Asit Kumar Haldar was initiated into art by a traditional *patua*, Jhareshwar Chakravarty. Training under Abanindranath Tagore at the Government School of Art, Calcutta, Haldar learned clay modelling from traditional artists Jadunath Pal and Bakkeshwar Pal, and sculpture from Leonard Jennings. One of the several artists to copy the Ajanta cave paintings, Haldar also worked on copying the Jogimara and Bagh cave paintings in central India. He became the first principal of Kala Bhavan, Santiniketan, where he taught from 1911 to 1923. He later served as the principal of the College of Arts and Crafts, Lucknow. In 1934, Haldar was elected a fellow of the Royal Society of Arts, London.

Untitled
Wash on paper, 31.5 x 24.5 cm

Debi Prasad Roy Choudhury
1899-1975

Debi Prasad Roy Choudhury was born in Tajhat in present-day Bangladesh. He learnt sculpting from Hiranmoy Roychoudhuri, painting from Abanindranath Tagore, and life drawing and portraiture from E. Boyess. Equally at ease with clay and paint, he cast sculptures in bronze and plaster, and painted using the wash technique while retaining a hint of realism. He was appointed the Superintendent of the Madras Art College, which he had first joined as a student, and the Indian government awarded him the Padma Bhushan in 1958. The Rabindra Bharati University honoured him with a D.Litt. in 1968. Choudhury's public sculptures are spread throughout the country, while his paintings are included in major national and international collections.

"Give with one hand and take away with the other" - it is a popular saying that means 'To act in a way that is helpful only to later do something to counteract or negate that initial action'. This sarcastic proverb is a perfect riposte to the majority of apparently 'benevolent' acts by the wealthy ruling class of 19th Century India.

Untitled
Watercolour on paper, 23 x 29 cm

Gaganendranath Tagore
1867-1938

A self-taught artist, Gaganendranath Tagore was the brother of Abanindranath Tagore and nephew of Nobel laureate Rabindranath Tagore. Beginning to paint at the age of thirty-eight, he played an important role in the establishment of the Indian Society of Oriental Art, Calcutta, in 1907. In the early years of his career, he painted Puri landscapes, portraits and other figurative sketches, scenes from Calcutta and illustrations for Rabindranath Tagore's *Jeevansmriti*. In 1914, six of his works were sent to London and then to the Pavilion Marson exhibition in Paris. It was after this that he introduced cubism in his works. He is known for the portfolio of cartoons *Birupa Bajra*, a merciless satire of contemporary Bengal society, and the witty caricatures of *Adbhut Lok*, published as *Realm of the Absurd*. The 1923 exhibition of his works in Berlin and Hamburg received praise from German critics for his modernistic outlook, expressionist tendencies and dynamic presentation of space.

Untitled, (Portrait of Rabindranath Tagore)
Ink, watercolour and pastel on paper, 26 x 17.75 cm

Untitled, (Landscape)
Watercolour on paper, 28 x 16.5 cm

Untitled, (Portrait of Nicholas Roerich)
Wash on paper, 19 x 15 cm

Untitled, (Caricature)
Lithograph, 24 x 18.5 cm

Untitled, (Gandhi)
Watercolour on paper, 24 x 18.5 cm

Kshitindranath Majumdar
1891-1975

Often called a 'saint-artist', Kshitindranath Majumdar was strongly influenced by Sri Chaitanya's Vaishnavism. He was trained in hymn-singing, interpreted legends from Indian epics and *Puranas*, and participated in drama productions. Majumdar became a student of Abanindranath Tagore and his newly-formed Indian Society of Oriental Art. Later, in 1912, he took over the responsibilities of teaching at the society with Nandalal Bose. Following Abanindranath's painting style, Majumdar took it further by inventing dresses and drapery for his figures that carried suggestions of Ajanta frescoes and Rajput paintings. His paintings are charged with his understanding of Bhakti and aim at a pure and transcendental expression through a filtering of hues achieved by his distinct wash technique. With this artist, called a Bhakta Shilipi by Abanindranath, ended the major phase of devotional art in the neo-Bengal 'School'.

Yashoda, despite not being the biological mother of Krishna, brought him up as a result of a great penance undertaken by her and her husband, Nanda in their previous lives. Krishna was a highly mischievous child and Yashoda would often be left worrying about his actions. This was part of Lord Krishna's 'Lila' (or divine play), but was rarely comprehended by the residents of Vrindavan where they lived.

Untitled
Watercolour on paper, 44.5 x 31.5 cm

Radha and Krishna's relationship falls beyond the purview of a typical romantic bond between an ordinary man and woman as is marked by complex feelings of obligation and intense yearning, for one another. Radha's connection to Krishna is thus one of a profound love that flows spontaneously, breaking everything that comes in its path - their union was depicted as a divine one.

Untitled, (Radha and Krishna)
Watercolour on paper, 42.5 x 32.5 cm

As the fable goes, Krishna and Radha are eternal lovers, who were together long before they descended on earth. Lotus is often attributed as a symbol of their delicate and unique love. To understand it, one has to understand the finer nuances of 'rasa' and 'prema' – that defined their indulgences during Krishna's time in Vrindavan.

Untitled, (Krishna Lila)
Watercolour on paper, 48 x 32 cm

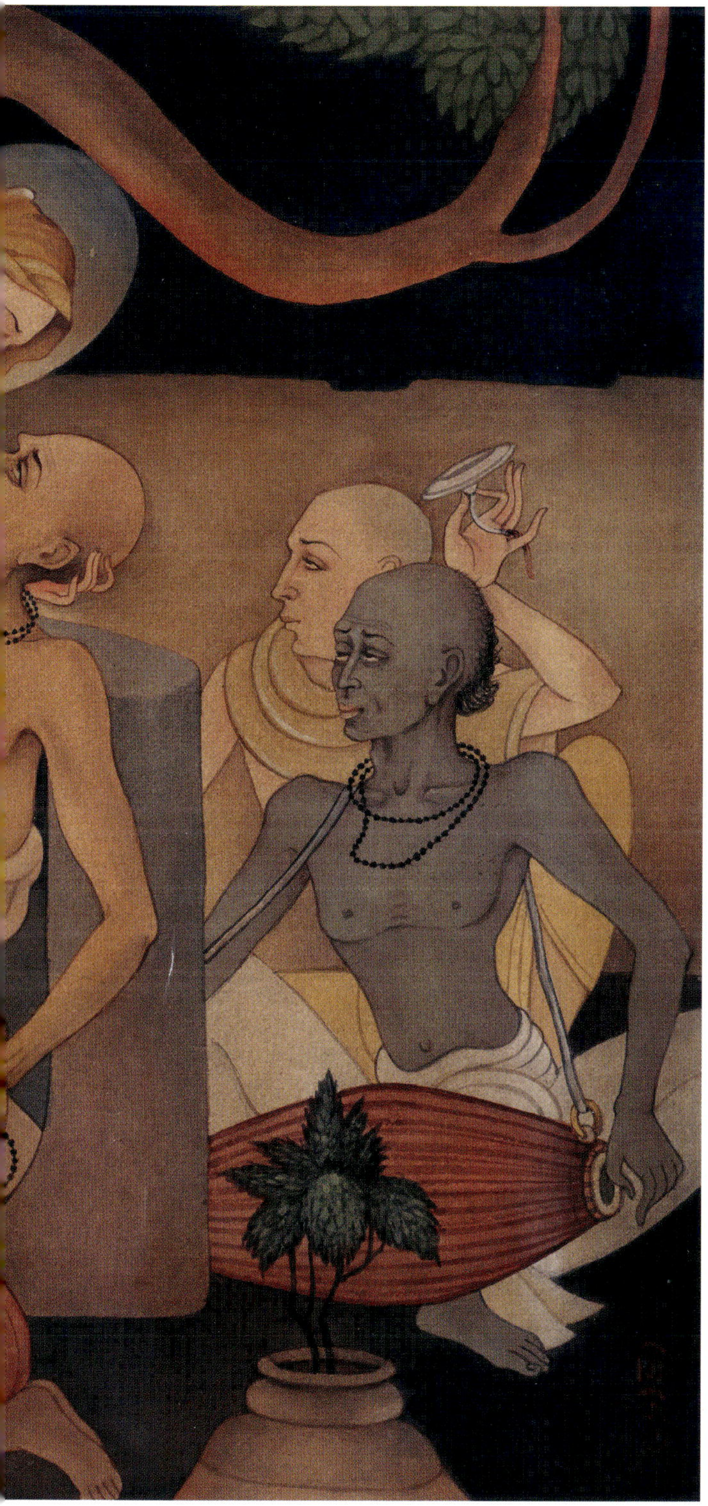

"Wake up! Having attained the human form of life, achieved self-realization and breaking out of the cycle of repeated birth and death" - this was one the famous spiritual realizations and preaching of Chaitanya Mahaprabhu that juxtaposed partially with Buddha's ideal. Lord Chaitanya is said to have the ability to communicate with the soul of a dying person and alleviate the dying person's pain. In Hinduism, it is customary to have priests and hymn singers create a pious environment around a dying man so that his last thoughts are that of God.

Untitled
Watercolour on paper, 33.5 x 50 cm

Nandalal Bose
1882-1966

Groomed initially by Abanindranath Tagore, Nandalal Bose drew early philosophical inspiration from Ananda Coomaraswamy, Sister Nivedita and E. B. Havell. Bose experimented with flat spaces seen in Mughal and Rajasthani miniatures, and incorporated Sino-Japanese styles in his washes. While working with Japanese painters at Calcutta and Santiniketan, he developed a calligraphic lyricism that became iconic to his painted line. In 1919, he joined Kala Bhavana, Santiniketan, as its first principal, mentoring a generation of artists such as the stalwarts Ramkinkar Baij and Benode Behari Mukherjee. Awarded the Padma Bhushan in 1954, his works were declared a National Art Treasure in 1972.

Untitled, (Ajanta)
Tempera on cloth, 37 x 32.5 cm

Untitled, (Ajanta Series)
Ink on paper, 19 x 14 cm

Untitled, (Village scene)
Ink on paper, 9.5 x 15 cm

Untitled, (Mahābhārata), 1952
Watercolour on paper, 50 x 74 cm

Bhishma was the grandfather of both the Pandavas and the Kauravas in the epic Mahābhārata. He was the commander of the Kauravas in the war against their cousins, the Pandavas. On the 9th day of the war, perturbed by Arjuna's inability to kill Bhishma which was costing a lot of damage to the Pandava army, Krishna jumped down from the chariot, picked up a wheel (opposed to his vow of never picking up a weapon in the war) and rushed to kill Bhishma.

Untitled, (Monk)
Watercolour on paper, 35 x 23 cm

Untitled, (Woman with Flower)
Watercolour on paper, 30.5 x 17.5 cm

Kaikeyee was the step mother of Rama. When Rama's coronation was announced, Kaikeyee's inherent reaction was that of pure joy. But her maid-servant, Manthara intoxicated her mind against this and convinced her that Rama's coronation would cause her own son to be deprived of his rightful place in the Kingdom. This ultimately led to Rama's 14 year exile.

Untitled, (Kaikeyee-o-Manthara "Kokka"), 1910
Japanese Woodblock print, 31 x 18 cm

Radhacharan Bagchi
1910-1977

Born in Pabna in present-day Bangladesh, Radhacharan Bagchi graduated from the College of Art and Craft, Calcutta, in traditional Indian art, oil painting and Western academism. In 1951, he joined Kala Bhavan at Santiniketan as a teacher, and went on to officiate twice as its principal. Bagchi enjoyed working in both tempera and oil, switching from one to the other with equal ease; he also worked with the graphic mediums of drypoint, etching, lithography and linocut. He was commissioned by Visva Bharati, Santiniketan, to paint a life size oil of Rabindranath Tagore and his family in 1961.

Untitled, (Santhal Dance)
Watercolour on paper, 45 x 43.5 cm

Chitrāngadā in Mahābhārata, was the daughter and only child of King Chitravahana of Manipur. Trained in warfare and fearless, she dressed as a warrior in male clothes. During his twelve years of exile, Arjuna encountered Chitrangada and fell in love with her, the moment depicted in this painting. When Arjuna approached the king to seek permission to marry Chitrāngadā, the king agreed on the condition that any male off-spring would remain behind to inherit the kingdom. As promised, Arjuna left after his heir, Babruvahana, was born and lost contact with his son until years later when both met on the battlefield, a calamity that ended in Arjuna's demise. The story is famously recounted in Rabindranath Tagore's play Chitra.

Untitled
Watercolour on paper, 49 x 34 cm

Ramgopal Vijayvargiya
1905-2003

Born in Baler in Rajasthan's Sawai Madhopur district, Ramgopal Vijayvargiya was initiated into painting at an early age by a wandering *sadhu* of the Ram Snehi sect. He joined the Maharaja School of Art and Craft in Jaipur, studying watercolour wash under S. N. Dey, a disciple of Abanindranath Tagore. Vijayvargiya is best known for paintings with Ajanta-like characteristics of graceful bodies, smiling mouths, doe-like eyes, sinuous arms and tapering fingers. He drew inspiration from Kalidasa's plays, the *Rāmāyaṇa* and the *Mahābhārata*, the medieval poet Bihari's *Satsai* and the Persian poetry of Omar Khayyam, Sadi and Hafiz. Unearthing traditional Rajasthani paintings led to his second body of work that featured vignettes of vividly coloured Rajasthani life. In 1984, Vijayvargiya was awarded the Padma Shri.

Untitled
Watercolour on paper, 25.5 x 16.5 cm

Untitled
Watercolour on paper, 25.5 x 15.5 cm

Sunayani Devi
1875-1962

Born in the Tagore family filled with talented writers and painters, Sunayani Devi was essentially a self-taught artist. A witness to the Bengal renaissance, it was only in her thirties that she began to paint, encouraged by her husband, the grandson of reformist Raja Ram Mohun Roy. Fascinated by devotional pictures as a child, the theme of her paintings revolved around the mythological and religious epics of Krishna Lila, the *Rāmāyaṇa* and the *Mahābhārata*, with her style highly influenced by Kalighat pat paintings. Sunayani had a deep unerring instinct for line and form, movement and rhythm and a vibrant imagination. Her works are striking for their simplicity and free flowing fine lines, highlighting the delicate features of the subject. Her colours are soft and vivid, with minimal details and ornamentation of subjects and setting. There is a vigour about her drawings and a naïve simplicity of colour and composition that is reminiscent of the best of Indian miniature paintings.

Untitled
Watercolour and tempera on paper, 30 x 24.5 cm

Untitled, (Woman with lotus)
Watercolour and tempera on paper, 25.5 x 21 cm

Untitled, (Shiva Parvati/Portrait)
Watercolour and tempera on paper,
23.5 x 19 cm/22.5 x 19 cm

Untitled
Watercolour and tempera on paper, 20 x 15 cm

Untitled
Watercolour and tempera on paper, 33 x 18 cm

Untitled, (Shiva Parvati)
Watercolour and tempera on paper, 23 x 22.5 cm

Untitled
Watercolour and tempera on paper, 29 x 22 cm

Untitled
Watercolour and tempera on paper, 20 x 7 cm

Abdur Rahman Chughtai
1894-1975

Born into a family of artists in Lahore, M. A. R. Chughtai learnt to draw from his father, Mia Karim Baksh. He obtained a diploma in photo lithography from the Mayo School of Art, Lahore, in 1914, before learning printmaking techniques and etching in London. He also apprenticed under Abanindranath Tagore in Calcutta and toured Europe from 1927 to 1931, holding solo shows. Despite post-Partition Pakistani claims on his heritage, Chughtai's contribution towards the art of the entire subcontinent is substantial; besides contributing towards resurrecting an Islamic cultural and political identity, he painted on eclectic subjects, ranging from Buddhist themes, Hindu epics and Radha-Krishna scenes, to illustrative paintings for the *Rubaiyat* of Omar Khayyam. Chughtai is Pakistan's national artist.

Untitled, (Extinguished Flame)
Watercolour on paper, 71 x 56 cm

Untitled, (Jahanara and the Taj)
Watercolour on paper, 76 x 54 cm

Bengal School Modernists

Later Bengal School artists observed the competing visions of Indian modern art. First, the western academic approach versus the orientalist Bengal School and, subsequently, the avante garde movement of our three rebels (Hemen Mazumdar, Rabindranath Tagore, and Jamini Roy).

These early modernists broke away from Western academic art as well as the nationalist, pan-Asian, Bengal School aesthetic. They also distanced themselves from traditional religious and mythological themes that had dominated centuries of Indian art.

Kalikinkar Ghosh Dastidar
1908-1972

Born in Gabha (Bangladesh), he was the founder member of The Young Artists Union, Calcutta in 1931 and the Founder member of The Art Rebel Center in 1933. He studied under the tutelage of Percy Brown, Govt. School of Art, Calcutta. Expelled from the college due to his association with the students revolution and strike during Mukul Deys tenure as principal. Later he joined the Govt. School of Art, Madras.

Rabindranath Tagore
Watercolour on paper, 16.5 x 12.5 cm

Benod Bihari Mukherjee
1904-1980

Born in Behala, Bengal, Benode Behari Mukherjee joined Santiniketan in 1917 and Kala Bhavana in 1919, where he was one of the first students of Nandalal Bose. A congenitally impaired vision that denied him normal schooling, brought him close to nature and had a deep impact on his art. Mukherjee renounced the overt symbolism of mythology in favour of themes from everyday life. Though he turned completely blind by the age of 50, he continued making drawings and small sculptures based on figural images achieved by folding paper. In 1973, Satyajit Ray made a documentary on his work, called *The Inner Eye*.

Untitled
Watercolour on paper, 36 x 27 cm

Chittaprosad Bhattacharya
1915-1978

A self-taught artist, poet, storyteller, and an active member of the Communist Party of India, Chittaprosad was inspired by village sculptors, artisans as well as puppeteers. In 1943-44, he experienced the Great Bengal Famine first-hand, resulting in his brutally honest depiction of human suffering in stark drawings and sketches made in pen and ink. Powerful and emotive, his art of caricature emerged as a statement in favour of the oppressed masses and as a denunciation of the ruling class. Apart from representing human suffering, the proletariat and the marginalised classes in his works, Chittaprosad also created landscapes and cityscapes, portraits, female figures, nudes and illustrations for books.

Untitled
Watercolour, pen and ink on paper, 28 x 33 cm

Gopal Ghose
1913-1980

An 'India wanderer', as he liked to call himself, Gopal Ghose was trained at the Maharaja School of Arts, Jaipur, and the Government College of Arts and Crafts, Madras. In 1943, he became one of the founder members of the Calcutta Group. During 1950-72, Ghose taught at the Government College of Art and Craft, Calcutta. Dexterous in handling different mediums, including watercolour, tempera, pen and ink, and pastels, Ghose became a legend in his lifetime for reinterpreting the genre of landscape painting.

Untitled, 1976
Watercolour, 35.5 x 48 cm

Untitled, 1945
Watercolour, 38 x 56 cm

Kartick Chandra Pyne
1931-2017

Kartick Chandra Pyne studied at the Calcutta Art College before joining the Society of Contemporary Artists in 1961. His paintings present a unique fusion of various art forms, whether adapted from native folk art or the stylistic innovations of the masters of modern art like Picasso, Matisse, Klee, Miró and Chagall. Depicting what he saw around him-nature and its beings-Pyne's focus was more on experimentation than on arriving at a fixed style. Deeply concerned with the internal world, Pyne was often identified as a surrealist.

Untitled, 1984
Ink on paper, 17.5 x 14 cm

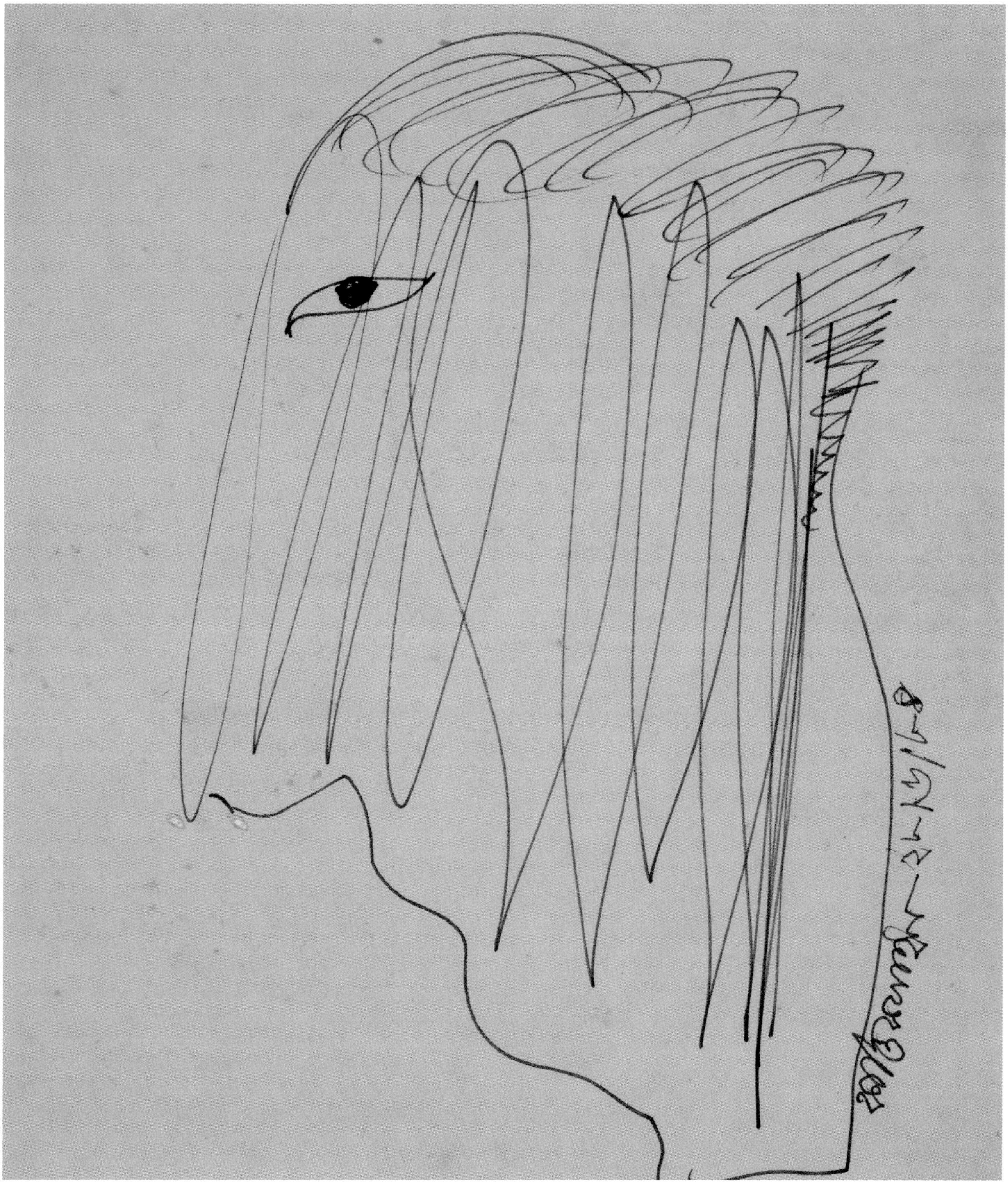

Quamrul Hassan
1921-1988

Quamrul Hassan is one of the pioneers of modern art in Bangladesh. His creative talents were multifaceted and his artworks are characterized by constant reinvention and experimentation. His ceaseless experimentation also facilitated a better understanding of the various media and their potential. Besides familiarity, this also gave him a facile competence in and control over diverse forms and expressions of art. A natural affinity for traditions lies at the heart of Quamrul's aesthetics. He has been eminently successful in blending the folk with with the modern, the indigenous with the western - creating a modern diction that retains its links to indigenous forms and expressions sustained over centuries. His works are distinctive because of this matchless blending of the arts and styles of the East and the West. There has been an additional embellishment at times by a measured touch of Chinese art.

Untitled, 1984
Ink on paper, 14 x 10 cm recto

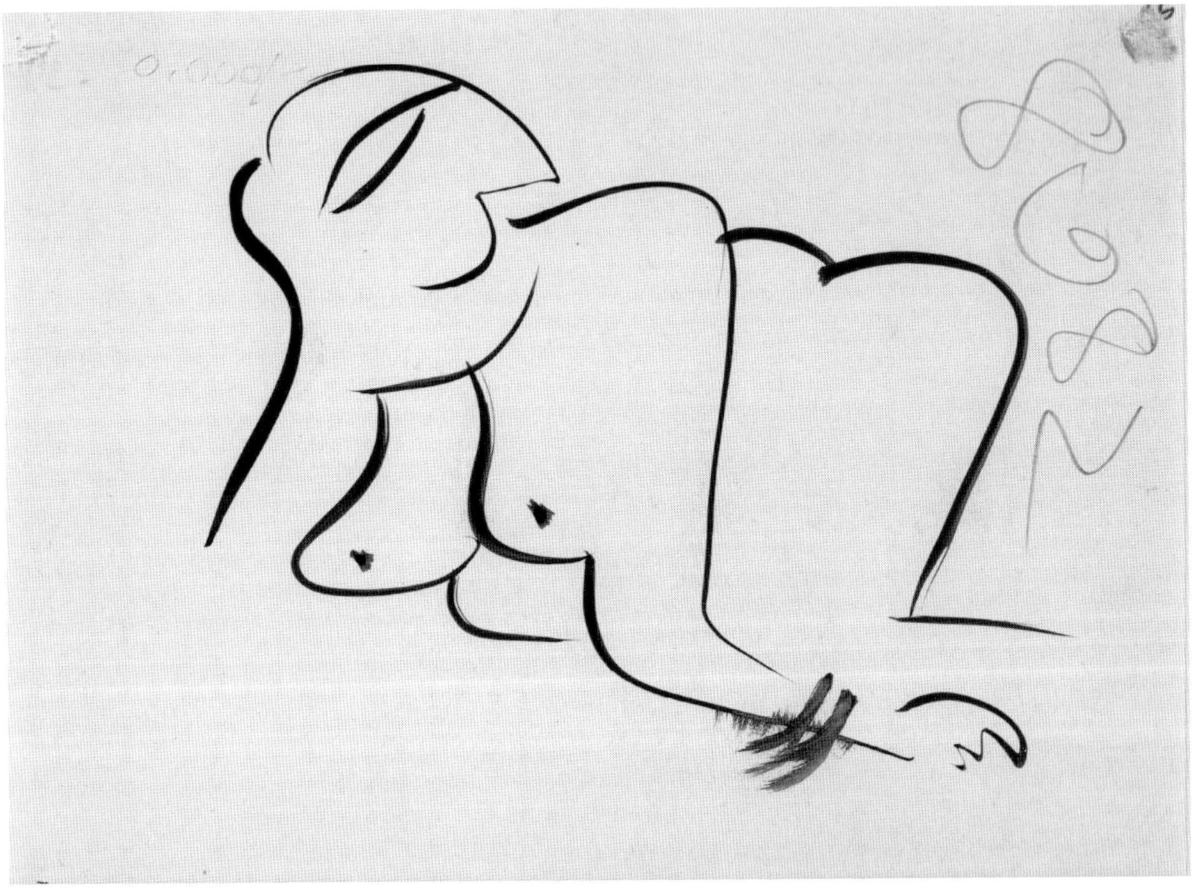

Untitled, 1984
Ink on paper, 10x14 cm recto and verso

Untitled, 1984
Ink on paper, 10x14 cm recto and verso

Untitled, 1985
Ink on paper, 9.75 x 6 cm

Untitled, 1985
Ink on paper, 9.75 x 6 cm

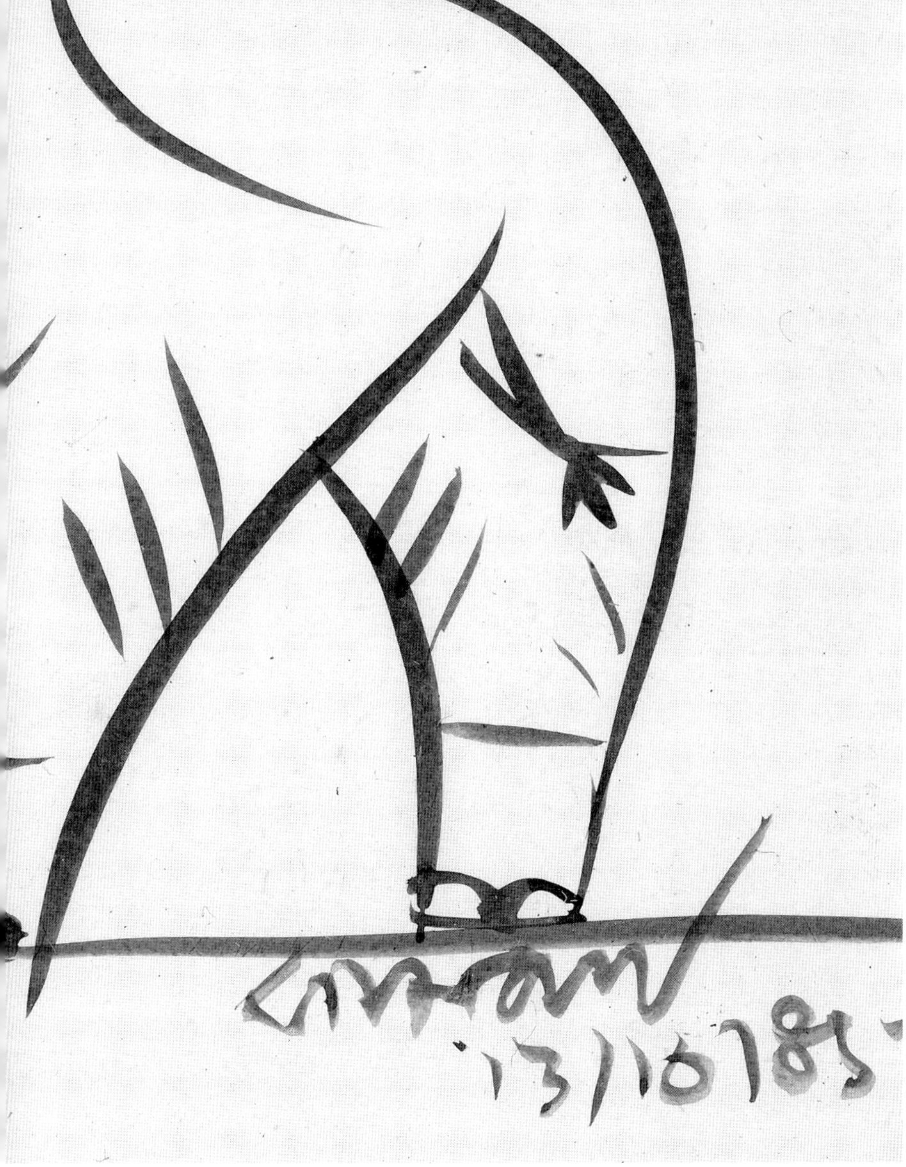

Untitled, 1985
Ink on paper, 6.5 x 9.5 cm

Untitled, 1983
Ink on paper, 23 x 32.5 cm

Ramkinkar Baij
1906-1980

An iconoclast who defied the artistic norms of Santiniketan, Ramkinkar Baij was the first artist to use oil paint and create distinctly modern and abstract works. Baij introduced concrete casting as an alternative to the more expensive plaster, stone or metal. A spontaneity of action was visible in his transparent watercolours and drawings, particularly in the sequence of nudes. The first truly 'modern' Indian sculptor, his work was monumental, and yet possessed an inner movement. The colossal *Yaksha* and *Yakshi* sculptures at the Reserve Bank of India, New Delhi, brought Baij widespread recognition. He was conferred the Padma Bhushan by the Government of India in 1970.

Untitled, 1948
Watercolour on paper, 24.5 x 35.5 cm

Untitled, 1960
Watercolour on paper, 25 x 19 cm

Untitled
Watercolour on paper, 32 x 38 cm

Somnath Hore
1921-2006

Studying briefly at the Government School of Art, Calcutta, in mid-1940s, Somnath Hore trained under painter Zainul Abedin, and printmaker Saifuddin Ahmed. A participatory, collective practice with fellow artists like Chittaprosad led to his intellectual growth. In a thirty-year teaching career, he set up the printmaking department of the Delhi Polytechnic of Art, and nurtured students at Kala Bhavan, Santiniketan. He was the quintessential Bengal artist deeply affected by the cataclysms that changed its social history, foregrounding in his works the working class and toiling peasant, grappling with issues of survival.

Untitled, 1985
Bronze sculpture, 61 x 30 x 10 cm

Lalit Mohan Sen

1898-1954

Lalit Mohan Sen took a diploma in painting from School of Arts and Crafts, Lucknow, in 1917, and joined it later as a teacher, eventually becoming its principal in 1945. In 1924, he joined the Royal College of Art, London, under a government scholarship to work with William Rothenstein. Here he gained expertise in portraiture and landscapes, murals, linocut and wood engraving. He was one of the four artists commissioned to paint frescos at India House, London. A disciple of Asit Haldar, Sen was also a good photographer and printmaker. He worked across media and his subjects spanned nationalism, the Indian middle class experience, village scenes and portraits. *Potter Girl*, wood engravings of Mahatma Gandhi and Rabindranath Tagore, and *Paniharin* are some of his better known works.

Untitled
Natural pigments on paper, 38 x 28 cm

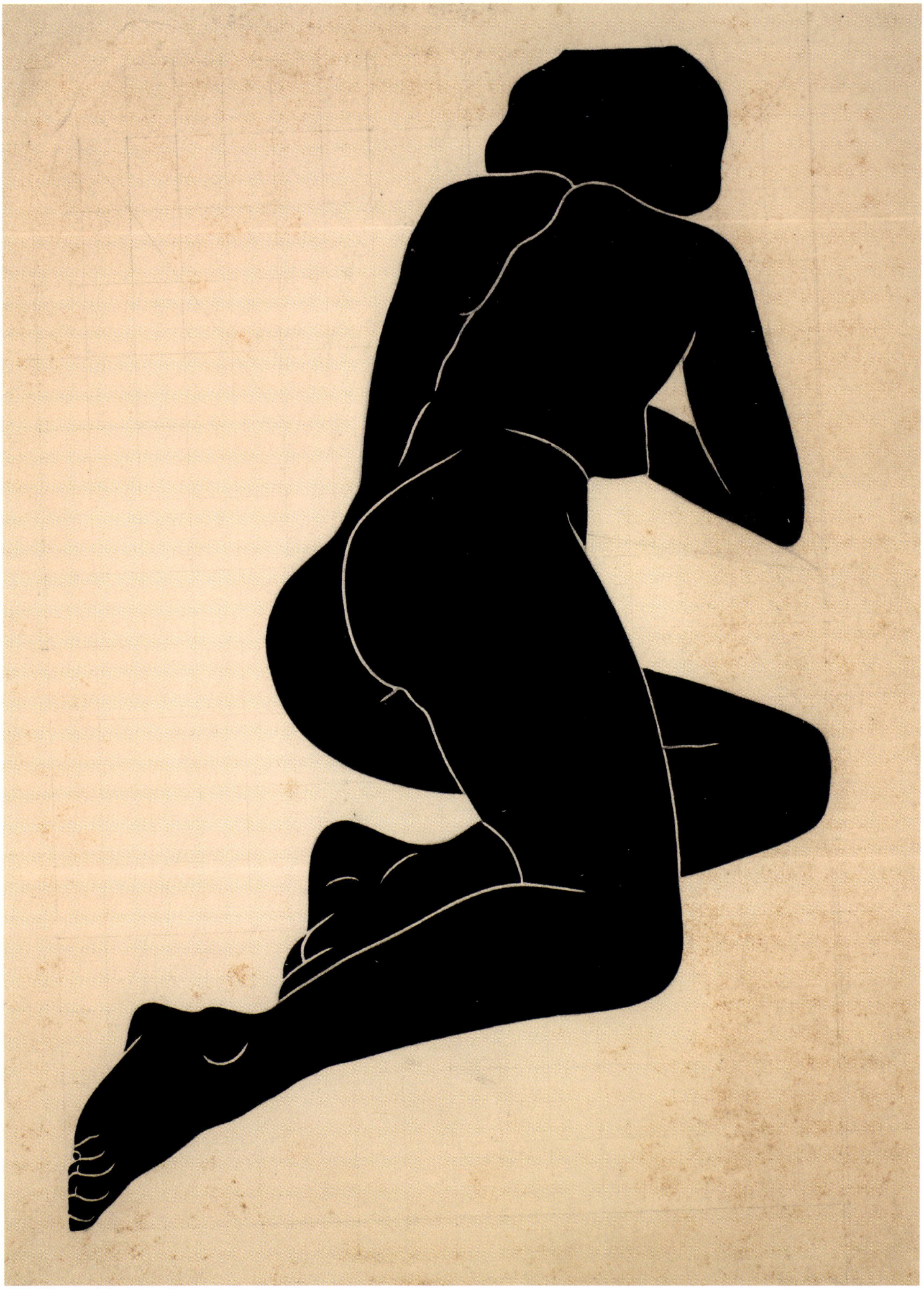

Untitled
Natural pigments on paper, 38 x 28 cm

Untitled, 1952
Pen and ink on paper, 38 x 28 cm

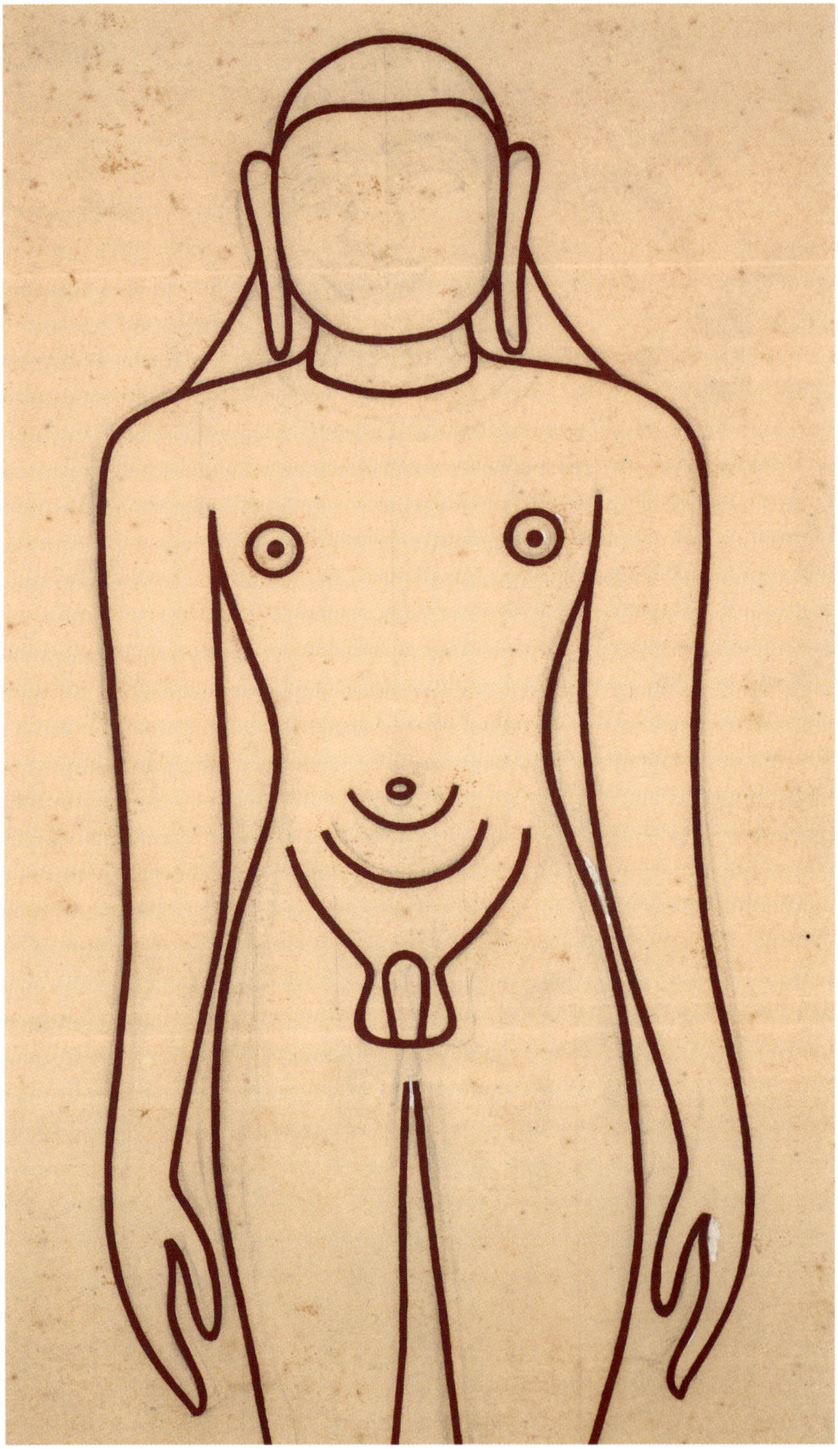

Untitled
Natural pigments on paper, 35.4 x 19 cm

Untitled
Natural pigments on paper, 38 x 28 cm

Untitled
Natural pigments on paper, 28 x 28 cm

Three Rebels
Rabindranath Tagore
Jamini Roy
Hemen Mazumdar

Rabindranath Tagore (1861-1941) became the first non-European Nobel Laureate, winning the Nobel Prize for Literature in 1913 for his book of poems Gitanjali. He took a keen interest in both Indian and Western contemporary arts. Seeing the new "Indian-style painting" falter in the hands of the Bengal School's lesser followers, Tagore put out a call for individualism: "...in the name of Indian art...we smother our souls under idiosyncrasies unearthed from buried centuries. I strongly urge our artists vehemently to deny their obligation carefully to produce something that can be labelled as Indian art according to some old-world mannerism. Let them proudly refuse to be herded into a pen like branded beasts". Tagore did not take up painting until he was well into his sixties after realising that there were some things he could not express in words. Developing doodles in his diaries into a distinctive expressionist style, his unschooled art remains an outpouring of his luxuriant imagination. In 1930, he became the first Indian artist to exhibit in Europe and the USA.

Jamini Roy (1887-1972) was the first Indian artist to fully break away from his training in Western naturalism. Instead he returned to his childhood vistas in rural Bengal. It re-ignited the compelling visual coda that had been impressed upon him through his early fascination with the folk decoration of a surface. Jamini Roy's contribution was the transformation of Bengal folk art and its elevation into an original and compelling modern art. Widely considered to be the father of modern Indian art, Jamini argued that "it was not possible for me to paint in the European way, nor in the Chinese or the Tibetan. To follow Persian or Mughal painting was similarly difficult for me...because I was not in their milieu... I do not care whether my paintings are good or bad. My sole desire is to make (them) look different."

Hemen Mazumdar's (1894-1948) lifelong artistic endeavour was to battle against the vision of the "Orientalist Bengal School". He favoured of a more universal language of art. Hemen famously wrote that the inability of the Bengal School to draw is camouflaged by their assertion of a 'spiritual' world beyond appearances. For him, this concept was an anathema to his rigorous formal practice.Hemen mature style is a harmonious marriage between East and West. His mastery of oil on canvas was used to render not historical subjects but to provide forbidden glimpses into the deeper recesses of upper-class Bengali households, particularly of its women. What had been prohibited by social mores suddenly seemed tantalisingly close. Hemen captured the ennui of the wealthy Bengali housewife, all but inaccessible to the public. His paintings, especially Pallipran, became the undeniable precursor to Bollywood's 'wet saree' scenes. It scandalised a society where nudity amongst the upper-classes was still very much taboo.

Rabindranath Tagore
1861-1941

Rabindranath Tagore was the youngest son of Debendranath Tagore, a leader of the Brahmo Samaj, which was a new religious sect in nineteenth-century Bengal. He was educated at home; and although at seventeen he was sent to England for formal schooling, he did not finish his studies there. In his mature years, in addition to his many-sided literary activities, he managed the family estates, a project which brought him into close touch with common humanity and increased his interest in social reforms. He also started an experimental school at Shantiniketan where he tried his Upanishadic ideals of education. Rabindranath Tagore was an icon of Indian culture. He was a poet, philosopher, musician, writer, and educationist. His painting style was very individual, characterized by simple bold forms and a rhythmic quality, and later served to inspire many modern Indian artists. Tagore's artistic adventure began with doodles. Crossed-out lines and words would take unplanned and accidental shapes, driven by intuitive decisions, usually budding from the memories of art and objects he saw in museums and books. Most of them represented animals but seldom the ones we know in reality; more often his doodles represented what he described as *"a probable animal that had unaccountably missed its chance of existence"* or *"a bird that only can soar in our dreams"*. Spurred by a spirit of inventiveness, his works merged the familiar with the unknown. Landscapes are the smallest output to Tagore's art. After he developed his love for painting, Tagore described the visible world around him *"as a vast procession of forms"*. As a child, he spent hours observing the forms of nature from his window. He derived a sense of companionship and support in the silent conversations he had with nature. The human face is a prominent constant in his artistic works and speaks of his undying interest in human persona. As a writer, Tagore linked human appearance with emotions and essence. He found a similar opportunity as a painter. His painted faces speak of vast human experience and intrinsic human emotion. Most of the women he painted are shown covering their hands and bodies under folds of their flowing veils or saris signifying the closeted existence of the Bengali women of his time.

Untitled
Watercolour on paper, 13.4 x 16.6 cm

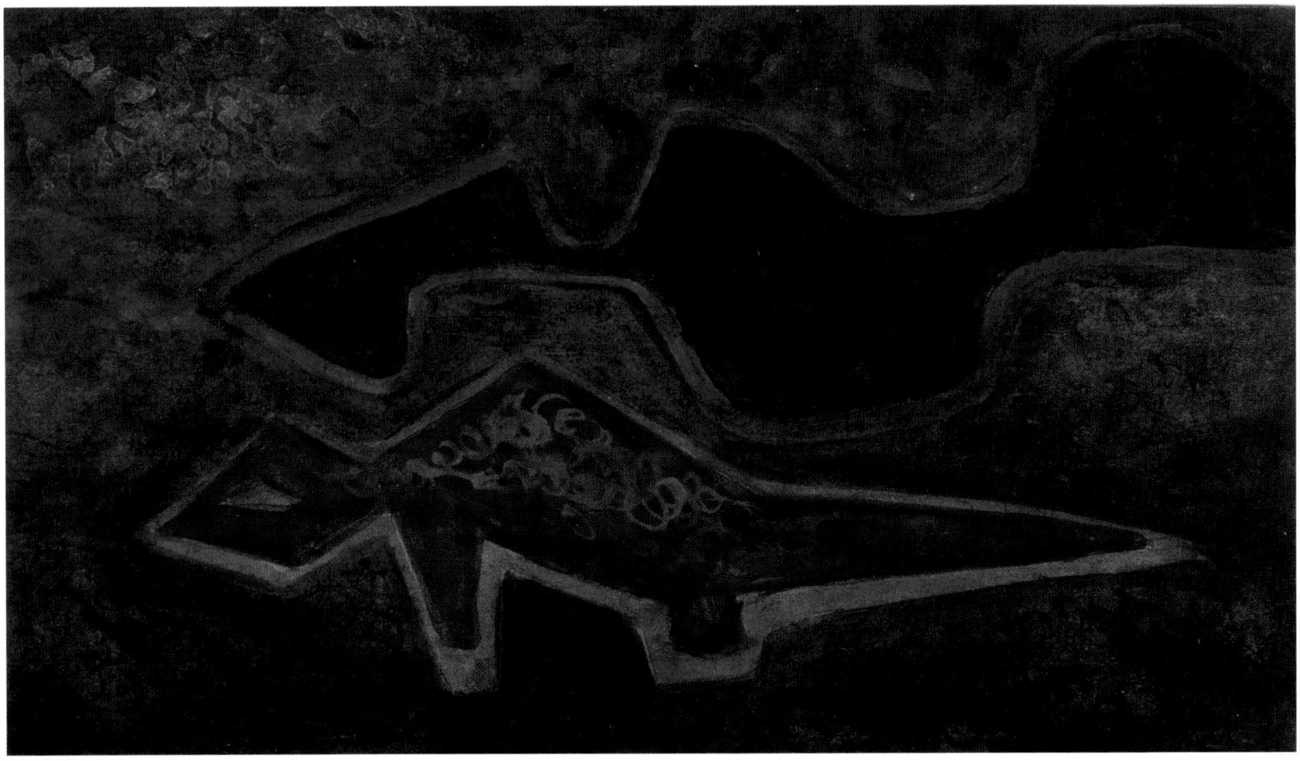

Untitled
Watercolour on paper, 26.7 x 44.5 cm

Untitled
Watercolour on paper, 12.4 x 21.4 cm

Untitled
Watercolour on paper, 16.4 x 23.7 cm

Untitled
Black & red ink
on handmade paper,
26.5 x 38.5 cm

Attributed to Rabindranath Tagore
Untitled, 1934
Watercolour on paper, 21 x 30 cm

Attributed to Rabindranath Tagore
Untitled, 1935
Ink on paper, 16.5 x 13 cm

Untitled, 1939
Watercolour and colored inks on paper, 40.5 x 25.5 cm

Attributed to Rabindranath Tagore
Untitled, 1938
Watercolour on paper, 38 x 28 cm

Attributed to Rabindranath Tagore
Untitled, 1936
Pastel on paper, 12.5 x 7.5 cm

Attributed to Rabindranath Tagore
Untitled
Watercolour on paper, 21 x 20 cm

Attributed to Rabindranath Tagore
Untitled, 1936
Watercolour on paper, 13.5 x 8.7 cm

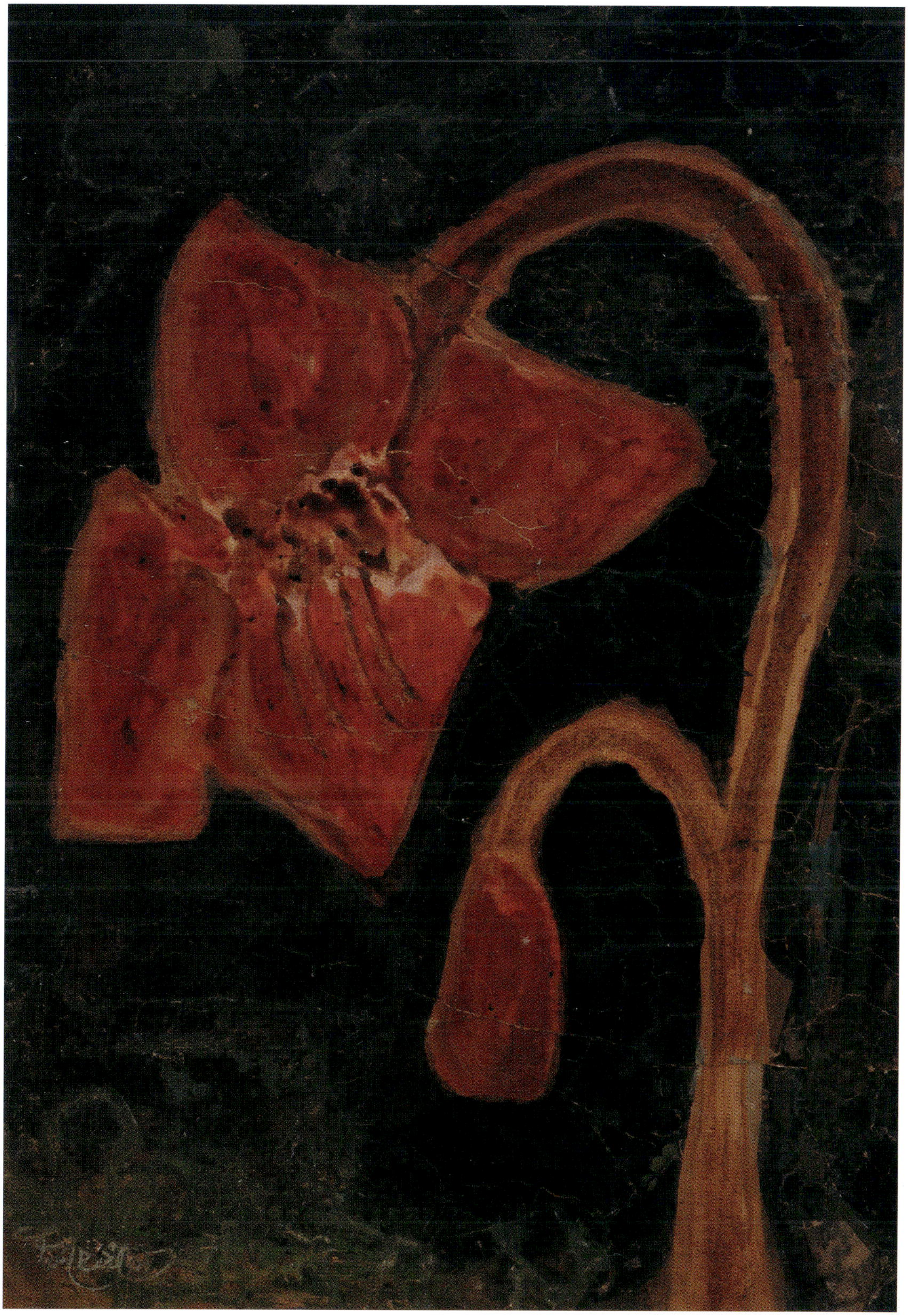

Attributed to Rabindranath Tagore
Untitled
Watercolour on paper, 25 x 17 cm

Jamini Roy
1887-1972

Jamini Roy was born in an affluent family of zamindars in the Beliatore village in the Bankura district, of then undivided Bengal. Rich in folk art tradition, the village played a dawning influence on the mind of this budding artist who found his true calling early in life. In 1903, at the age of sixteen, he moved to Calcutta to join the Government College of Art, where Abanindranath Tagore, the founder of Bengal School, served as the Vice Principal. Under Tagore's guidance, he learned the basic nuances of fine arts. He adhered to the age-old academic tradition of the institution of learning to draw classical nudes and oil painting. Following five years of training, he received his Diploma in Fine Arts in 1908.

Jamini Roy was one of the most influential painters of the 20th century, who through his work gave expression to the true essence of Bengali folk art. Preferring to call himself a patua, his technique and subject matter was influenced by the traditional Indian folk and village art, particularly the one found in Bengal. What made him distinct from other painters of his generation was his admonishment of modernity professed by art-schools and instead switching over to Indian roots, tradition and culture for inspiration. With time, he developed his own amazing style that was akin to indigenous art found in Kalighat street paintings. All his paintings boasted of having rhythmic outlining, neat pattern, bright earthy shades and daring simplicity of themes. Roy was not only responsible for making art accessible to all but also for highlighting the true identity of Indian art.

Jamini Roy's life as artist extends over four decades, between the 1920's and the mid 1960's. At first blush the most characteristic elements to note are two. On the one hand, his legendary productivity, which led him to produce over twenty thousand works, created uninterruptedly even until his last years, marked by illness and old age. On the other hand, the way in which his human and artistic trajectory was entirely superimposed to the complex political social and economic history leading to the independence of India (1947) and to the progressive assertion, despite all internal and external tensions, of a modern national cultural identity. Those meanings, linked to the historical context in which his life occurred, are of such relevance that for a long time, in the absence of other deeper analyses, they have provided the main themes of the critical narratives on Jamini Roy's oeuvre.

Untitled, (Woman), 1935 ca.
Tempera on paper, 37.5 x 28.5 cm

Untitled, (Blue Figure with Parrot), 1940 ca.
Gouache on canvas, 94 x 49.2 cm

Untitled, (Nude Lady), 1915 ca.
Tempera on canvas, 42 x 33 cm

Untitled, (Santhal Girl - Flower), 1912 ca.
Tempera on card, 73.7 x 47 cm

Untitled, (Ghats on the Hoogly River), 1915 ca.
Gouache on paper, 37.5 x 54 cm

Untitled, (House), 1915 ca.
Tempera on paper, 34 x 46 cm

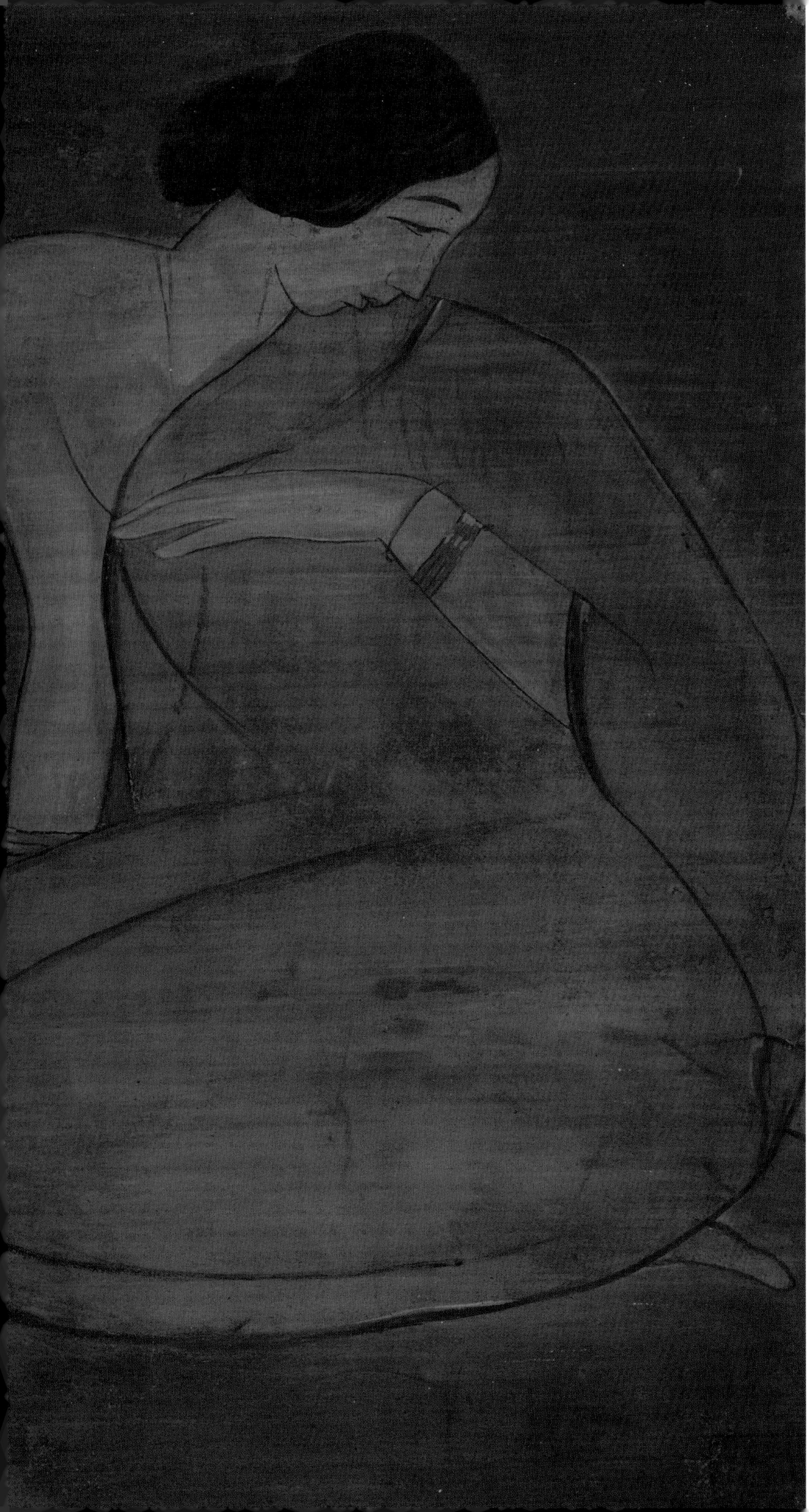

Untitled, 1920
(Seated Woman)
Tempera on cloth,
81.5 x 44.5 cm

Untitled, (Seated Woman), 1965 ca.
Tempera on card, 40 x 25.2 cm

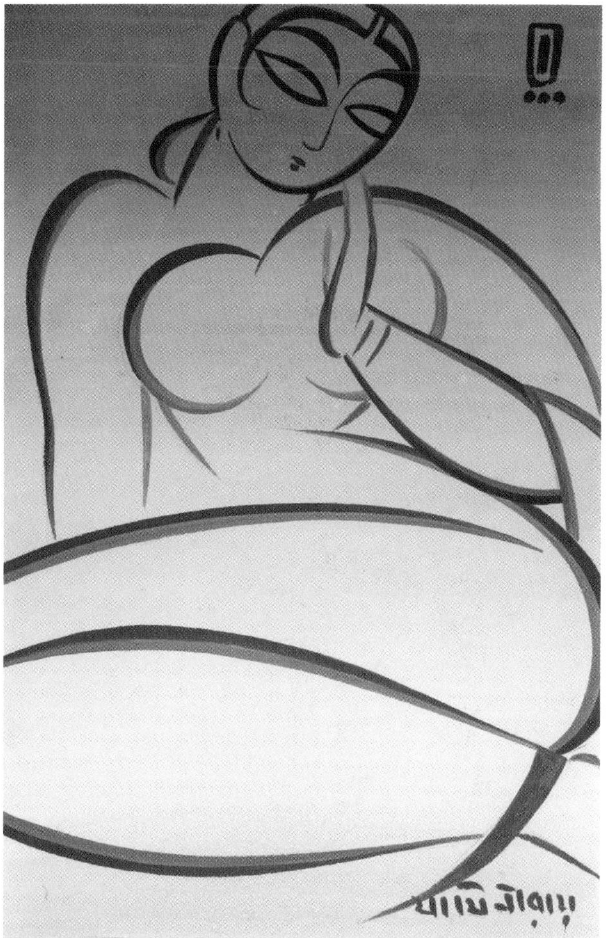

Untitled, 1950 ca.
Tempera on board, 40 x 30 cm

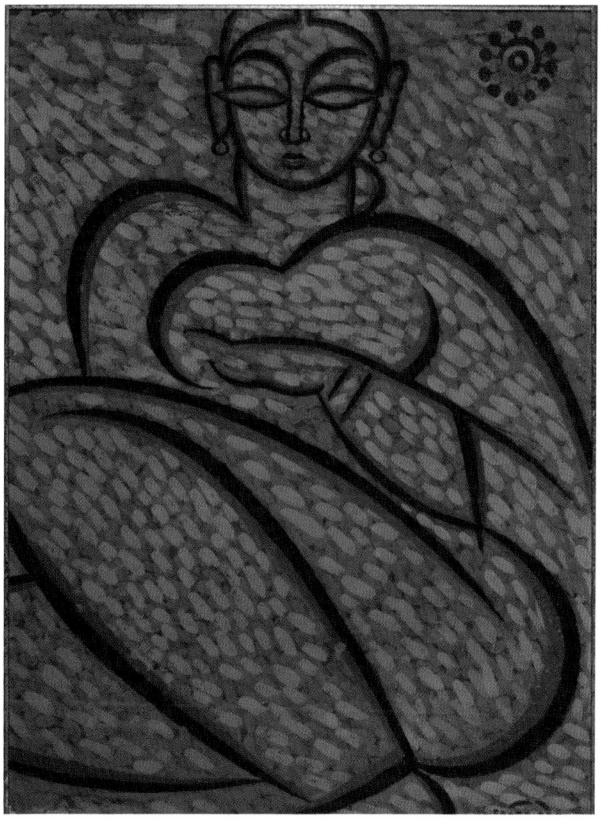

Untitled, (Gopini), 1965 ca.
Tempera on cloth, 85.5 x 45.7 cm

Untitled, (Woman Dancing), 1920 ca.
Tempera on cloth, 77.5 x 57.2 cm

Untitled, (Three Women), 1940 ca.
Gouache on paper, 73.6 x 40 cm

Three Women, 1950 ca.
Tempera on paper, 67 x 39 cm

Untitled, (Mother and Child), 1950 ca.
Tempera on card, 43 x 28.5 cm

Untitled, (Widow), 1940 ca.
Tempera on paper, 77.2 x 36.6 cm

Untitled, (Woman's Face), 1965 ca.
Tempera on card, 33.5 x 25 cm

Untitled, (Mother), 1965 ca.
Tempera on paper, 66 x 35 cm

Untitled, (Three Dancing Ladies), 1950 ca.
Tempera on paper laid on board, 39.4 x 72.1 cm

Untitled, 1945 ca.
Tempera on paper, 76 x 38.5 cm

Untitled, (Santhal Drummers), 1940 ca.
Tempera on card, Recto: 39.4 x 28 cm

Untitled, (Santhal Musicians), 1953 ca.
Tempera on card, 48 x 57.5 cm

Untitled, (Ganesh and Parvati), 1940 ca.
Tempera on card, 48 x 34 cm

Untitled, (Krishna playing flute), 1950 ca.
Tempera on board, 42 x 32 cm

Untitled, (Cat holding Kitten), 1955 ca.
Painting on board, 39.5 x 41 cm

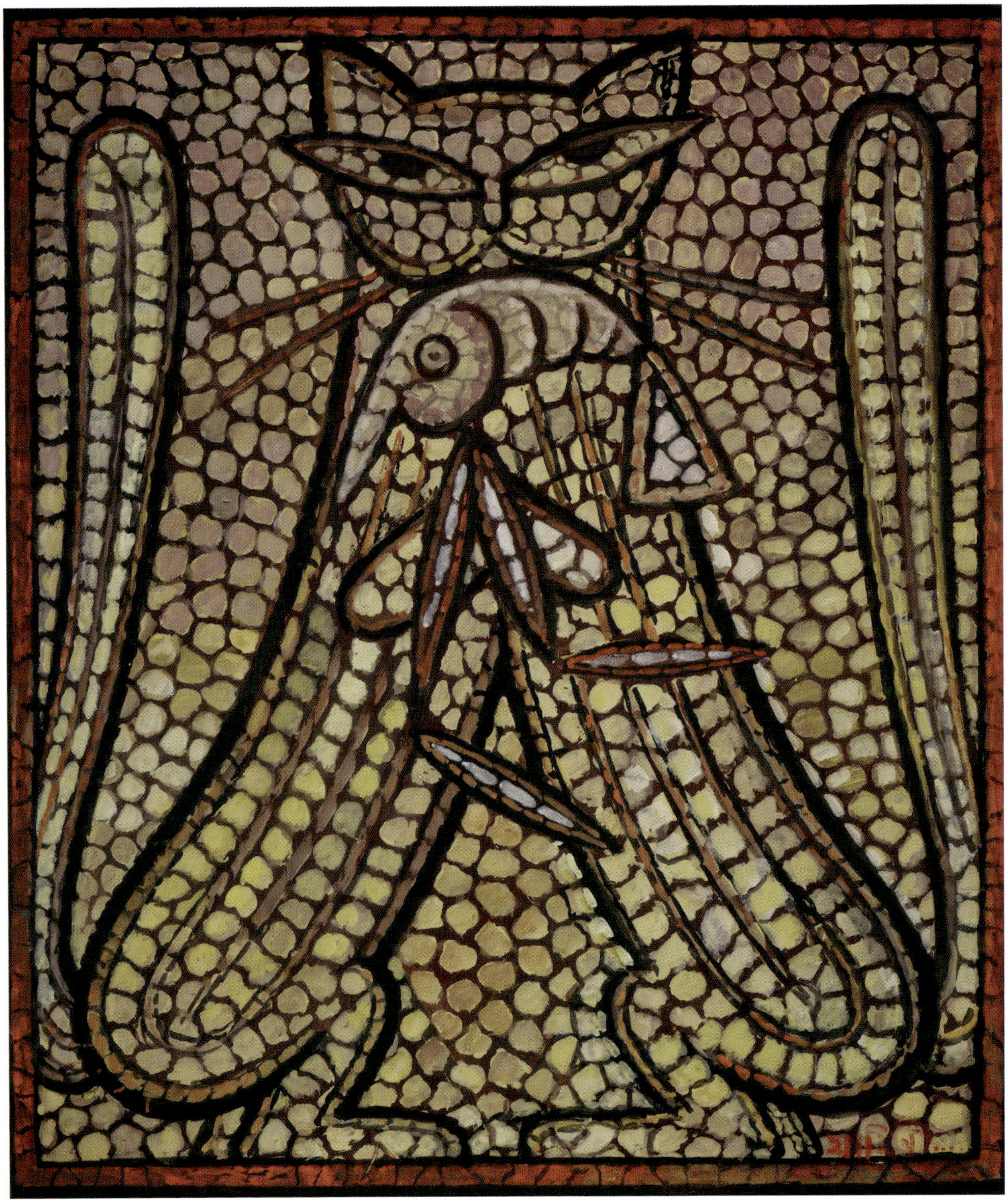

Untitled, (Cat with Crayfish), 1940 ca.
Tempera on paper, 77 x 65 cm

Untitled, (Two cats with lobster), 1940 ca.
Tempera on card, 42 x 31 cm

Untitled, (A Recumbent Cat), 1940 ca.
Ink and opaque colour on card, 28 x 43 cm

Untitled, (Yellow Bell - Cow and Calf), 1955 ca.
Tempera on board, 38 x 49 cm

Untitled, (Bull), 1950 ca.
Gouache on card, 32.8 x 39.2 cm

Untitled, (Rider on Horse), 1955 ca.
Tempera on board, 33 x 46.5 cm

Untitled, (Abduction of Sita), 1955 ca.
Tempera on paper, 38.1 x 48.9 cm

Untitled, 1950 ca.
Tempera on board, 22 x 70 cm

Untitled, (Krishna and Balarama), 1950 ca.
Gouache on linen, 86,7 x 148 cm

Untitled, 1940 ca.
Tempera on woven paper, 73.7 x 38 cm

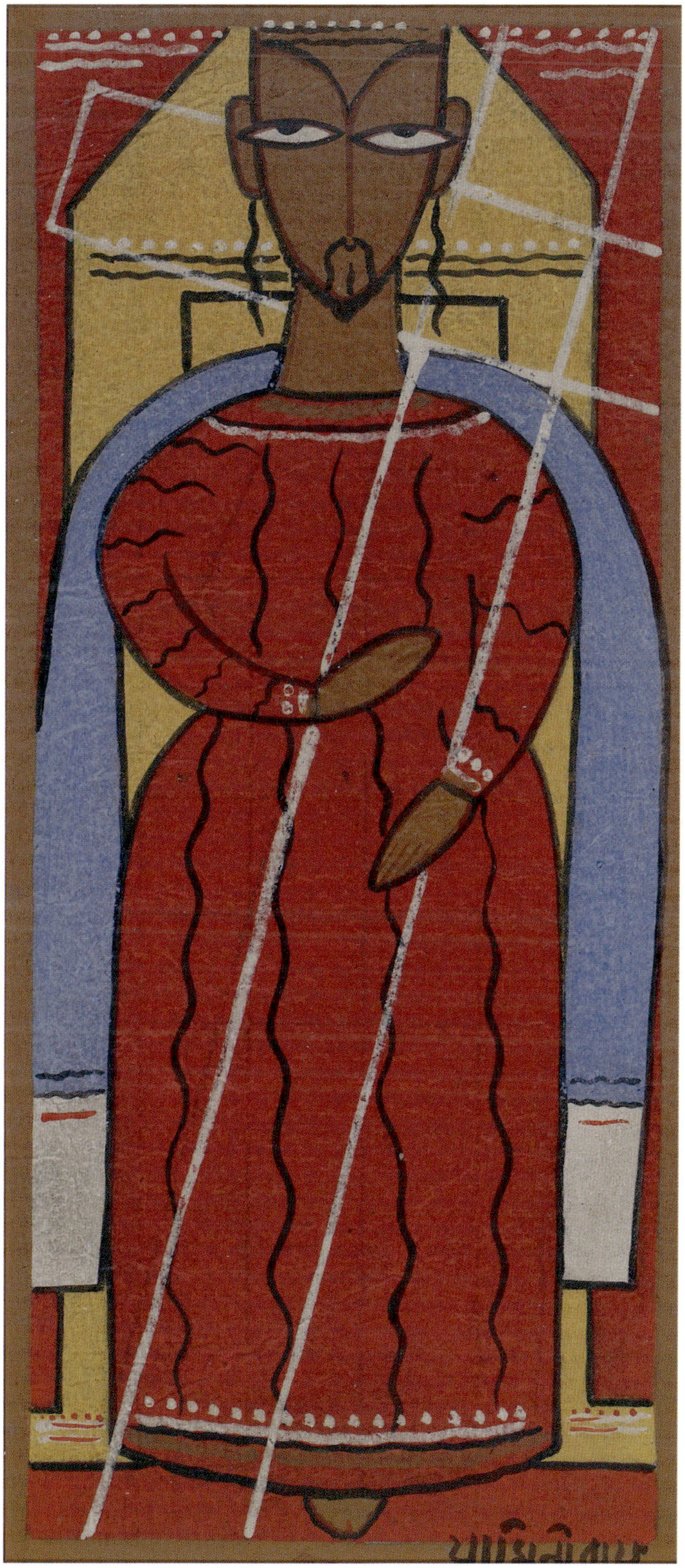

Untitled, (Jesus Christ), 1955 ca.
Watercolour on card, 35 x 15 cm

Untitled, (Last Supper), mid 1950s ca.
Tempera on card, 25.8 x 74.5 cm

Untitled, (Flight to Egypt), mid 1950s ca.
Oil on canvas, 63 x 84 cm

যামিনী রায়

Untitled, (Rabindranath Tagore/Christ), 1950 ca.
Tempera on board, Recto: 30.5 x 21.5 cm

Untitled, (Rabindranath Tagore/Christ), 1950s
Tempera on board, Recto: 30.5 x 21.5 cm

Untitled,
(Portrait of Rabindranath Tagore), 1930 ca.
Tempera on card, 30 x 39 cm

Hemendranath Mazumdar
1894-1948

Hemendranath Mazumdar, popularly referred to as Hemen Mazumdar, was born 1894 in Gachihata village of Mymensingh district, which is currently part of Bangladesh. Coming from a relatively wealthy landowning family, at the age of sixteen, Hemen dropped out of school and ran away to Calcutta to pursue his passion for painting. His early exposure to art seems to have been entirely through illustrations that appeared in magazines and books. He enrolled at the Government College of Art in 1911. The Government College of Art that Hemen entered had undergone a remarkable transformation over the previous fifteen years. It had evolved from an institution "established by a benevolent government for the purpose of revealing to the Indians the superiority of European art." Under the successive leadership of Ernest Havell, Abanindranath Tagore, and Percy Brown, the college had moved away from mandating students to copy western academic art as part of their training to espousing Indian art as the basis of the curriculum.Frustrated by abandonment of western academic tenets in instruction, Hemen left Government College of Art in 1912 for another institution in the city. Jubilee Art Academy was sympathetic to academic naturalism, but Hemen was more self-taught with the help of art books he sourced from overseas. By 1915, he left Jubilee Art Academy to start earning his living through portrait painting. The 1920s helped establish Hemen Mazumdar as a major Indian artist with a national reputation. Starting in 1920, Hemen won the gold medal at the annual exhibition of Bombay Art Society for three consecutive years. From 1930, for the rest of his life, Hemen Mazumdar remained a celebrated Indian artist. His popularity attracted the attention of Indian royalty. Among his patrons were Maharajas of Bikaner, Cooch Behar, Dholpur, Jaipur, Jodhpur, Kashmir, Kotah, Mayurbhanj, and Patiala. At each of these courts, he painted the portraits of the royal family. After the death of Maharaja of Patiala in 1938, Hemen returned to Bengal. He set up studios in Calcutta as well as the Dhiren Studio in Hooghly district under the patronage of the local zamindar. After participating in the All India Exhibition at Eden Gardens, Calcutta, Hemen Mazumdar died on 22 July 1948.

Daydream, 1930s
Oil on canvas, 115.5 x 84.7

Attributed to Hemendranath Mazumdar
Untitled, 1930s
Oil on canvas, 158 x 114 cm

Finishing Touch, 1930s
Oil on Canvas, 108.5 x 72 cm

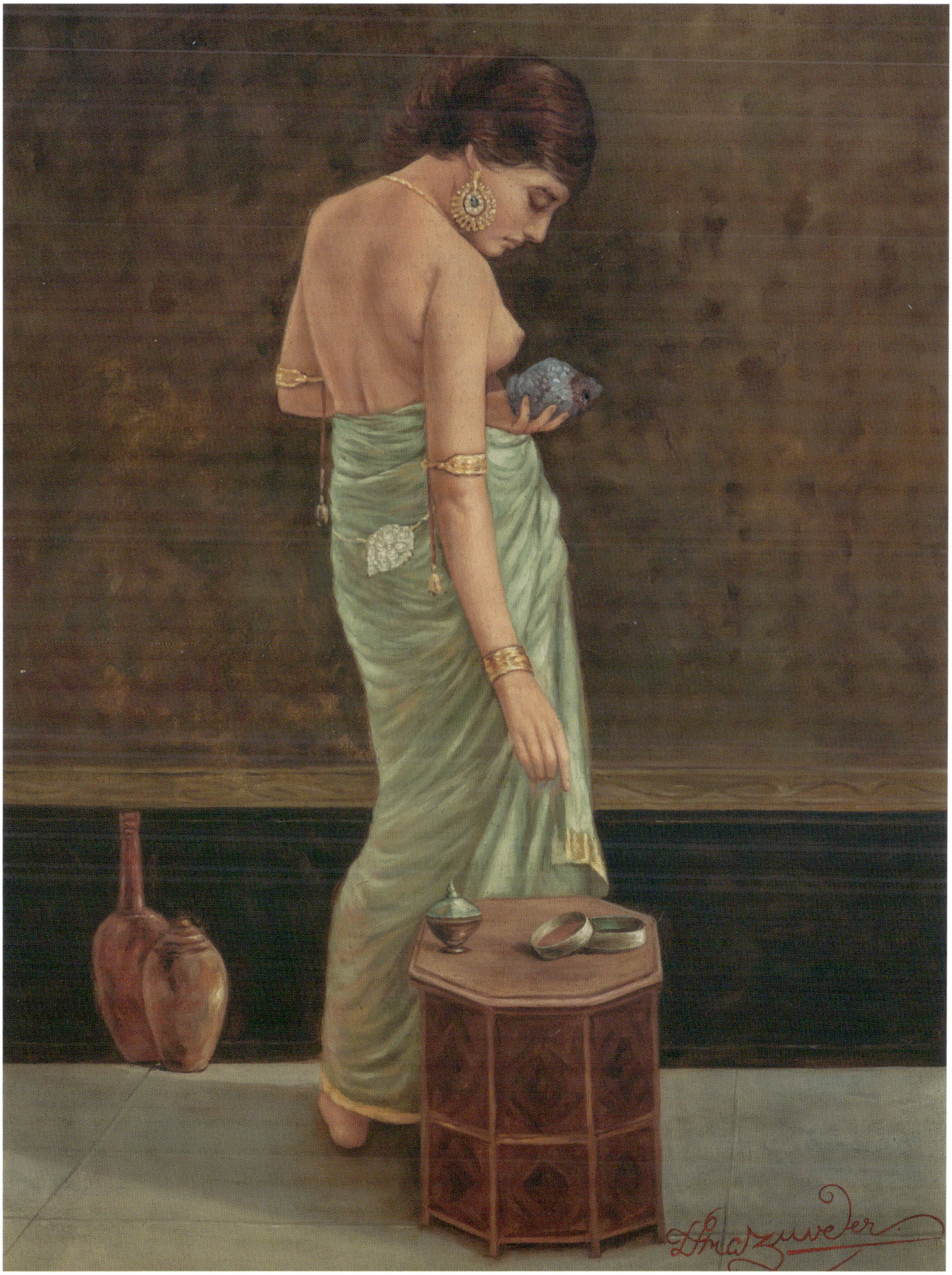

Shilpi, 1930s
Oil on canvas, 74.5 x 53.3 cm

Untitled, 1930s
Watercolour on paper, 40 x 28.5 cm

Image, 1930s
Oil on canvas, 86.4 x 60.3 cm

Wounded Vanity, 1930s
Oil on canvas, 86 x 60.4 cm

Harmony, 1930s
Oil on canvas, 79.4 x 59.2 cm

In Expectation, 1930s
Oil on canvas, 114 x 75.5 cm

Untitled, 1930s
Oil on canvas, 78 x 57 cm

Secret Memory, 1930s
Watercolour on paper, 33.5 x 27.3 cm

Ear-Ring, 1930s
Watercolour on paper, 37 x 25 cm

Untitled, 1930s
Watercolour on paper, 36 x 25.5 cm

Ear-Ring, 1930s
Oil on board, 71 x 55.6 cm

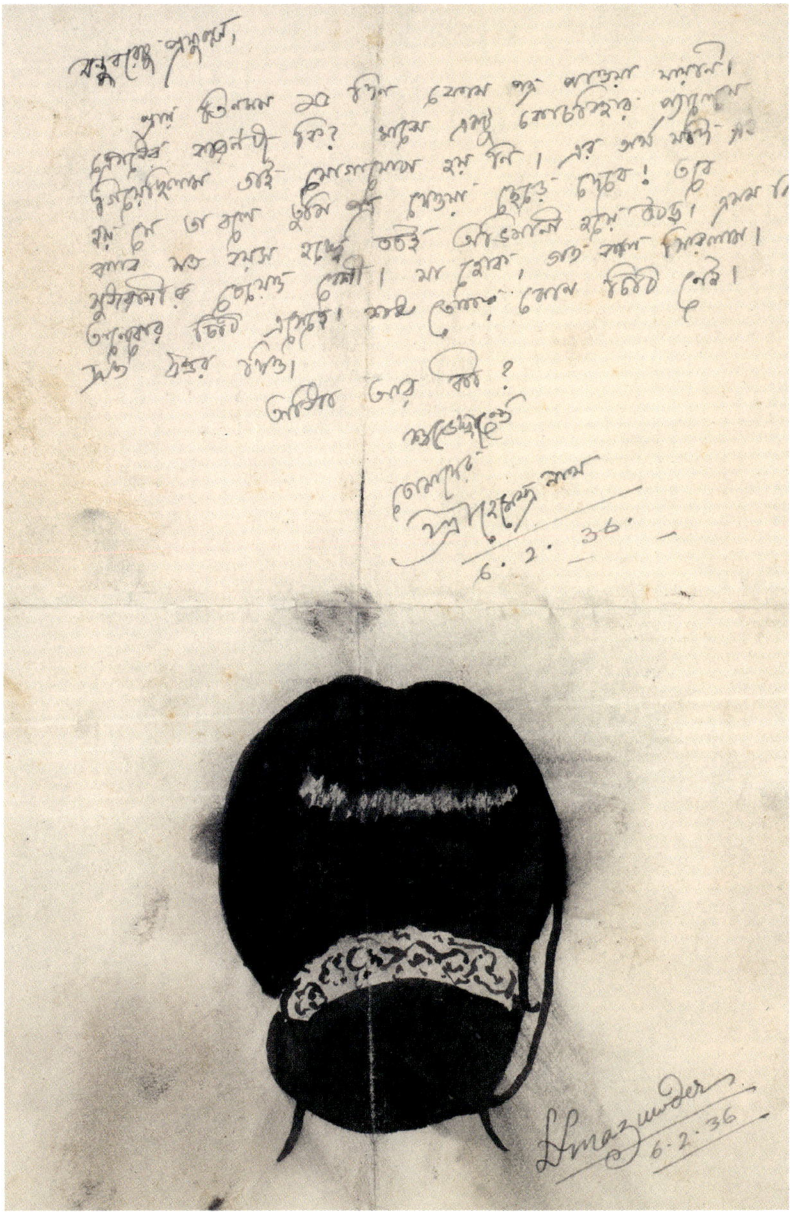

Untitled, 1936
Pen and ink on paper, 21.5 x 13.5 cm

Untitled, 1930s
Watercolour on paper, 31 x 23 cm

Untitled, 1930s
Ink on paper, 20 x 31.7 cm

Dilli ka laddu, 1930s
Crayon on paper, 20.8 x 15.4 cm

Dilli ka laddu, 1930s
Watercolour on paper, 36 x 25 cm

Dilli ka laddu, 1930s
Oil on canvas, 79 x 49.2 cm

Untitled, 1930s
Oil on canvas, 102 x 61 cm

Untitled, 1930s
Oil on canvas, 90.5 x 61 cm

Pallipran, 1930s
Oil on canvas, 90.3 x 61.5 cm

Monsoon, 1930s
Oil on canvas, 109.2 x 155.4 cm

Monsoon, 1930s
Watercolour on paper, 25.5 x 36.7 cm

Passing Cloud, 1930s
Oil on canvas, 90.7 x 60.6 cm

Untitled, 1930s
Oil on canvas, 91 x 61.5 cm

The First Sight, 1930s
Oil on canvas, 96 x 142.6 cm

Rose or Thorn, 1930s
Oil on canvas, 61 x 50.7 cm

Blue Swari, 1930s
Oil on canvas, 90.5 x 62 cm

Spirit of Maidenhood, 1930s
Watercolour on paper, 32.5 x 23.3 cm

Untitled, 1930s
Watercolour on paper, 37.5 x 25.7 cm

Spirit of Maidenhood, 1930s
Oil on canvas, 89.5 x 55.5 cm

Untitled, 1930s
Oil on canvas, 90.5 x 60.6 cm

Caterina Corni (b. 1979) has a master's degree in Art History and Criticism from the Università Statale di Milano, her thesis was about the contemporary Indian artist Subodh Gupta. She began her career by cooperating with the journal "Flash Art". At the same time she worked as curator, and organized temporary exhibitions in Europe, the United States, the United Arab Emirates and in India. Since 2004, her interests have turned in particular to modern and contemporary Indian art and to the study of the relationships and interactions between Western and Oriental art. She has edited the catalogues for several monographs and collective exhibitions. In 2014, her project on the relationship between Indian artist Jivya Soma Mashe and Israeli artist Michal Rovner, was selected by the Centre Pompidou (Paris) for the XXV anniversary of the exhibition "Magiciens de la Terre". Caterina Corni is an Associate Professor of Art History at Symbiosis University, Pune and she is also a Member of Assemblea degli Afferenti of the Centre for Cultural Heritage Studies, Università dell'Insubria.

Dr **Daniel Rycroft** is Senior Lecturer in the Arts and Cultures of Asia at the University of East Anglia. He is Postgraduate Course Director in the Department of Art History and World Art Studies, which is where he has been teaching since 2006. He is author of Representing Rebellion, editor of The Politics of Belonging in India, editor of World Art and the Legacies of Colonial Violence, and founder of the journal World Art. He has also co-convened the Santal Rebellion 150 Forum, co-founded the South Asian Arts Group, and is currently chair of UEA's India Dialogue. As part of this Dialogue, he co-directs UEA's Humanities in India Partnerships Programme.

Isabelle Kent is an art historian, curator and lecturer specialising in early modern European art. She is currently a PhD candidate at Trinity College, University of Cambridge, with a focus on the visual culture of Spain and Latin America. Her publications include Collecting Murillo in Britain and Ireland (editor and contributor, 2020), as well as various articles and reviews in the Burlington Magazine, Hispanic Research Journal and Apollo Magazine. From 2017 to 2019 she was the inaugural Enriqueta Harris Frankfort Curatorial Fellow at the Wallace Collection, and has previously worked at the Metropolitan Museum of Art, British Museum and Dulwich Picture Gallery. She holds a BA and MPhil in History of Art from the University of Cambridge.

Nirmalya Kumar is passionate supporter of Indian art. Previously a patron of British Museum, he has also served on the South Asian Acquisition Committee for Tate Modern. Over three decades, his collection of Bengal School, 1900-1950, has focused on Jamini Roy (considered to be the father of Indian modern art), Hemen Mazumdar (primary exponent of academic realism in Indian art) and Rabindranath Tagore (Nobel laureate 1913), Nirmalya frequently lends works to exhibitions. In 2014, BBC Radio 4 aired a 30 minute documentary on his London collection entitled "From Bengal to Baker Street". In 2015, the Museo Delle Culture in Lugano Switzerland curated a Jamini Roy exhibition with 65 works from his collection. In 2019, Singapore Management University hosted Hemen Mazumdar: The Last Romantic based on 36 works from his Singapore collection. For his contributions to South Asian art, the School of Oriental and African Studies (SOAS) awarded Nirmalya an honorary fellowship in 2012. In his professional life, Nirmalya is Lee Kong Chian Professor of Marketing at Singapore Management University and Distinguished Fellow at INSEAD Emerging Markets Institute. Prior to this, heading strategy as Member-Group Executive Council at Tata Sons, he reported to Cyrus Mistry, the Chairman for the $100 billion Tata group. Professor Kumar previously taught at Columbia University, Harvard Business School, IMD (Switzerland), London Business School, and Northwestern University (Kellogg School of Management). He has also appeared on the 50 Best B-School professors in the world and 50 most influential Business School professors.

Shilpi Das is a PhD candidate at Kazi Nazrul University, India. Having completed her MA in English literature in 2015, she began her doctoral research on unearthing and exploring the artistic contributions of women artists of twentieth-century Bengal. With a focus on women artists of twentieth-century India, she has presented her research papers at the Indian Institute of Advanced Study (IIAS, Shimla, India) in 2018 and Edinburgh College of Art (University of Edinburgh, Scotland) in 2019. She has also presented her papers centring on Indian art history at IGNCA (Indira Gandhi National Centre for the Arts, Delhi), University of Dhaka (Bangladesh), CWDS (Centre for Women's Development Studies, Delhi) and Ireland India Institute (Dublin City University, Ireland). Her book review of Art and independence: YG Srimati and the Indian Style and Meera Mukherjee: Purity of Vision has been published in the December 2020 issue of Studies in People's History. Her latest publications include Women, Buddhism, Nationalism: A Study in their Inter-relation through Asitkumar Haldar's A Panorama of the Life of Lord Buddha (published in Women and Buddhism: Perspectives on Gender, Culture and Empowerment by IGNCA in 2019), The Bengal School's Unsung Women Artists (published in the December 2020 issue of Marg magazine). She is also actively engaged in translations of art and artist-centric texts. Co-authored with Dr Santanu Banerjee, her translation of Chitranibha Chowdhury's essay on Nandalal Bose entitled In the Bower of Art has been published in Art in Translation (Volume 12. 1, July 2020). She has future plans to unveil more about the forgotten female artistic geniuses of Indian art.

Sona Datta is an art historian and cultural collaborator who until recently was Head of South Asian art at the Peabody Essex Museum in Massachusetts where she extended the museum's world-renowned modern Indian collections to include the best contemporary art referencing all of South Asia. Sona previously worked at the British Museum for 8 years where her exhibitions included the flagship Voices of Bengal season (2006), which attracted more people of South Asian extraction than any project in the British Museum's history. Sona also radically redefined the British Museum's engagement with modern collecting through the acquisition of contemporary art from Pakistan that linked to the Museum's holdings of historic Mughal painting. In 2015, she wrote and presented BBC4's Treasures of the Indus, described as an 'adventure with engaging historical and cultural material and lifting the veil on the region's past showing you must know where you have been to know where you are going'. Sona graduated with a First from King's College, Cambridge University and was awarded the prestigious Rylands Prize for Excellence in the History of Art. Her new book is a radical revision of South Asian art that will reset the lens on the so-called 'East'. She lives in London with her husband, two boys (and no dog).

Acknowledgments

Contributors
- Dr. Daniel Rycroft, University of East Anglia
- Isabelle Kent, London
- Shilpi Das, Shantiniketan

Supporters
- Betty Yao for her kind introduction to Leicester Museum
- Bashir Mohamed, London
- Elimijn Sanders, Leuven
- Imma Ramos, British Museum, London
- Maya Prarthana Berggren Kumar, Lausanne
- Mehreen Rizvi-Khursheed, London
- Rubaba Dowla, Dhaka
- Sumitra & Prakash Kejriwal, Kolkata
- Suseela Yesudian, Little Chalfont

Technical Assistance
- Ansa Picture Framing & Art Gallery, Singapore
- Benaka Art Conservation, Singapore
- DAG, Delhi: Ashish Anand and Kishore Singh for artist bios
- Ginevra Carrai, Italy
- Giulia Belloro, Graphic designer, Italy
- Graham Bignell Studio, London
- J. Manley Gallery, Eton
- Justin Piperger, Photographer, London
- Pratirupa Sarkar, India
- Ruey Loon Ung, Photographer, Singapore
- Simonetta Caporale and Chris Gilmour for translating "The Aesthetics of Contamination", Caterina Corni

Leicester Museum
- Chris Kirby
- Claire Cooper
- Harjeet Kaur
- Simon Watkins
- Marketing and retail teams

9 788894 592085

50 GBP